The Nitty Gritty of
Mortgage Backed Securities

"Empower your litigation. Expose foreclosure fraud."

BY

RICHARD MERRILL KAHN

Written by one of America's top testifying experts in the field of securitization and foreclosure fraud.

http://www.NittyGrittyOfMBS.com

Published By

Forensic Professionals Group U.S.A, Inc.

http://www.FPG-USA.com
"Mortgage Analysis as Part of a Credible Defense against Foreclosure"
Serving all 50 States

"The Nitty Gritty Of Mortgage Backed Securities "

"Empower your litigation. Expose foreclosure fraud."

Published by

Forensic Professionals Group U.S.A, Inc.

http://www.FPG-USA.com

ISBN: 973-0692776247

Manufactured in the United States of America

About the Author

Richard Kahn has had a professional career in mortgage analysis, residential and commercial real estate, mortgage backed securities and lender financing that has spanned more than thirty years and billions of dollars in equity and mortgages. He has extensive experience in courts including County, State (from Circuit to Supreme), and Federal (from District to Appeals) including Federal Bankruptcy and Appeals. He is FPG-USA's qualifying expert witness on all FPG-USA issuances. Mr. Kahn has held licenses in securities, real estate, and mortgage finance.

EXPERIENCE

1973 through 1977

I began my professional career on Wall Street for Merrill Lynch. There I was involved with one of C.E.O. Donald Regan's projects, appointed in the capacity of National Real Estate Tax Shelter Product Manager of Merrill Lynch. (This is the same Mr. Regan who went on in 1981 to become the 66th United States Treasury Secretary in President Ronald Reagan's Administration and then became White House Chief of Staff.) While at Merrill Lynch, I analyzed, structured and handled billions of dollars in mortgage backed securities and syndicated real estate investments across Merrill's base which included six thousand account executives.

1978 through 1994

I was C.E.O. and a founding partner of Affiliated Real Estate Analysts (AREA). At AREA, we structured, reviewed and analyzed mortgage backed securities, real estate transactions, commercial mortgage financing, as well as performed lender compliance analysis and forensic discovery in a fiduciary capacity.

1995 through 2008

I was principal broker and partner in residential and commercial real estate mortgage lending. This included private funding as well as Government Sponsored Enterprise (Fannie Mae, Freddie Mac), originating and underwriting loan originations for sale into the secondary marketplace. During this time I also taught a monthly 3 day lender licensing course in a prestigious mortgage lender licensing school for 2 years.

2008 through Present

I am Director and Senior Qualifying Mortgage Analyst of Forensic Professionals Group USA, Inc, DBA FPG-USA (fpg-usa.com). FPG-USA provides securitization and forensic loan audit services to attorneys nationwide. Attorneys use FPG-USA investigative services to research and report genuine issues of material facts that exist for pleadings and trial and to direct Judicial notice to facts and documents in the evidentiary process.). I am FPG-USA's qualifying expert witness on issuances created for submission into evidence across State and

Federal Courts. I offer oral testimony to support my evidentiary findings.

I have provided written testimony in many hundreds of cases, involving over 160 lenders. I have performed work on cases across many States, including Alabama, Arizona, California, Colorado, Connecticut, Delaware, Florida, Georgia, Hawaii, Idaho, Illinois, Indiana, Iowa, Maine, Maryland, Massachusetts, Michigan, Minnesota, Missouri, Montana, Nebraska, New Hampshire, New Jersey, Nevada, New Mexico, New York, North Carolina, Ohio, Oklahoma, Oregon, Pennsylvania, Tennessee, Texas, Utah, Virginia, Washington and Wisconsin.

I have provided oral testimony in cases on the witness stand and/or in deposition testimony on dozens of occasions including on cases in Arizona, Colorado, Idaho, New York, Oregon, Pennsylvania and multiple cases across multiple counties in Florida including Monroe, Dade, Broward, Palm Beach, Saint Lucie and Santa Rosa.

I have developed and utilize a unique method and process to investigate, obtain evidence and material facts, analyze and research in the process of FPG-USA business. I have created, authored and presented over 240 individual sessions and 119 customized topical library videos, teaching my particular methods of mortgage foreclosure fraud and securitization auditing and investigation.

I have personal knowledge of and have written the entire content of this book personally. I am able to testify to the matters stated herein. I provide my written and oral testimony in the cases I perform investigations and report on issues for use in court. I readily appear and testify before the Court, including on issues presented herein.

PROFESSIONAL LICENSES HELD

FL Correspondent Mortgage Lender Licensing 2004-2009

FL Mortgage Broker: Initial license 1995.Status: Current; ???

FL. Real Estate Broker Initial 1995. Status Current

NY Real Estate Broker Initial 1986 Status: Expired

Series 7 SEC NYSE NASD Securities and CBOE Commodities Licensing.

Initial 1974. NASD Last: 1995

PERSONAL ACHEIVEMENTS

- Single engine private pilot (ret.) with 3,000 hours, of which 1,000 were IFR instrument flight.

- 3rd Dan Black Belt in Kenpo martial arts, still practicing. National karate team competitor for 7 years (from age 33 to 40) amassing 220+ amateur rounds in judged competition, resulting in over 70 trophies and medals including Regional Champion, National Champion and Amateur International Champion in class for fighting and forms.

- Inducted into the Martial Arts Hall of Honors 2013.

Author's Acknowledgement

I would like to thank my wonderful wife and children for their loving devotion. Also for their cooperation during this last month and a half, allowing me to work crazy hours to accomplish the writing of this book.

I'd like to thank The Almighty for health, love happiness and the time to enjoy it. With health we can tackle life's challenges with a strong positive mental attitude. We can work hard for what we believe in.

I'd like to thank my many hundreds of clients including law firms and borrowers whom I have been blessed to have worked for and continue to work for as their testifying expert of record in their cases.

I'd like to especially thank my clients who have given me time this month and last to set their work orders aside and concentrate full time on writing this book. Without their consideration I would not have been able to accomplish this.

I'd like to thank the litigators, on both sides and the Judges who I have had the honor of appearing for, or against, and have been judged by. The Judicial System in America is the backbone on which our Constitution relies. These are the fighters and referee of our ring.

Nitty Gritty of MBS © 2016 Richard M. Kahn

TABLE OF CONTENTS

INTRODUCTION

Millions of homeowners in the United States have obtained mortgages destined to default. Their mortgages were used as a commodity to earn their original lenders and subsequent buyers two three and four or more times the mortgage amount in profits within weeks of the loan origination. In the process the loans were fully paid off multiple times over. Predatory loan servicers have and are creating falsified documentation, fabricating false affidavits and recording them in county records and Court to win foreclosure of homes they don't own, don't have a dime loaned out to the borrower and don't represent anyone who can lawfully prove they own the loan.

I am a testifying expert for the borrower side in wrongful foreclosure in many hundreds of cases nationwide providing securitization, mortgage lending and mortgage foreclosure fraud investigations, findings and testimony for borrowers and their attorneys in contested foreclosure litigation and forced loan modification settlement.

When President William "Bill" Clinton signed the repeal of the Banking Act of 1933 in November 1999, fourteen months before he left office he enabled commercial and mortgage bankers to again get in cahoots with investment bankers that fostered and created the mortgage meltdown of 2008 and the financial crisis. With his signature tens of millions of Americans have lost their homes and jobs. The big banks benefited, the economy suffers. America is $20 trillion dollars in debt. He knew the consequences. President Roosevelt, America's only 4 term president and his administration put those regulations in place to prevent what caused the Great Depression. This was the legacy Clinton gave America as he exited office.

Banks created Mortgage Backed Securities ("MBS") that collapsed financial markets, destroyed our booming economy. Unscrupulous loan servicing successors of these same lenders now seek to foreclose on homes whose mortgages were paid off in spades. They create fabricated claims of ownership which does not exist to win these homes for themselves as a windfall because they don't have a dime loaned out on the mortgages they are attempting to foreclose.

A network of foreclosure litigation attorneys around the Country has discovered this and contests these wrongful foreclosures nationwide. Attorneys and those they represent cannot offer substantive testimony in their own cases, all they can do is allege. So many seek to find a qualifying expert to investigate, report and testify. The Author has performed many hundreds of these investigations and issued testimony in cases taking place across the USA.

The issue behind these thefts is Mortgage Backed Securitization ("MBS"), a complex financial engineering of mortgages into certificates of ownership that trade like stocks, and caused mortgages to be originated and sold for astronomical profits. Foreclosure severs the responsibility of the originating and successor parties that profited so loan modifications are nil and foreclosure by any means is the only target on their horizon. They mock our courts as they mocked the American people in causing economic disaster, they are following it up with stealing many American's homes as their exit strategy of greed and profits on the backs of unknowing homeowners.

I've been asked hundreds of times about the nitty gritty of MBS in my professional career. On the witness stand, in deposition, by borrowers, borrower's counsel, opposing counsel and judges. I've decided to put the topics and explanations in writing for the benefit of those litigating this terrible dilemma and desperate for the truth. Within the covers of this book you will discover facts and information underlying the most intriguing and monumental financial scam in history. A scheme that dwarfs that of the Great Depression a hundred fold. One that has put tens of millions of Americans out of work, out of their homes and collapsed the entire economy, leaving America in unimaginable debt and beholden to the foreign enterprises and governments that now own America, its people and enterprises as our bankers. The information herein is offered empower those exposing mortgage foreclosure fraud litigated in court. , MBS Securitization is at the root of its creation and existence.

Nitty Gritty of MBS © 2016 Richard M. Kahn

Chapter 1

Deregulation gives birth to the nightmare of MBS Securitization

Neatly summed up, MBS securitization is the financial engineering of mortgages by commercial mortgage bankers, into securities sold to investors by Wall Street investment bankers.

Exactly the type of enterprise the Banking Act of 1933 prohibited.

The Introduction touched on changes in mortgage practices since 2000 that created MBS securitization. In November 1999, just 14 months before leaving office, democratic President William "Bill" Clinton signed the repeal of the Banking Act of 1933 into law. This Deregulation fathered the onslaught of toxic MBS securitization.

The Banking Act of 1933 kept commercial and investment banks apart. It was created by Carter Glass in 1933, an American politician. The Glass-Steagall Act is also commonly known as the Banking Act of 1933. It was named for the two Democratic congressman who sponsored it. So here we have it, in 1933 it was Democrats who closed the Pandora's Box. 66 years later it was a Democratic president who opened it.

In 1913, 20 years prior to the creation of the Banking Act of 1933, Carter Glass sponsored the Glass-Owen Act that created the Federal Reserve System. Carter Glass went on to serve as Secretary of the Treasury under President Woodrow Wilson. Treasury Secretaries are individuals with marked financial genius.

Before the Banking Act of 1933, the marriage of commercial banks and investment banks precipitated The Great Depression. Let's go back for a brief moment, to that fateful month of November 1999 that repealed it.

Then President William "Bill" Clinton was enjoying his last 14 months in office. The 106th Congress was made up of a Republican majority in the House and Senate. Clinton was to hand over the reins around January 21, 2001. The 106th Congress would hand over their reins around January 4, 2001. The president taking office on January 21, 2001 was George W. Bush. Clinton had battled an impeachment trial that spanned five weeks during January and February of 1999. With the impeachment over, the Dow Jones closed above 10,000 for the first time in history on March 29, 1999. And it remained that way in Clinton's last year in office.

In November 1999, the Y2K bug was the media darling. The repeal of the Banking Act of 1933 took backstage. In hindsight, the Y2K bug was nothing but a hiccup and the repeal of the Banking Act of 1933 marked the birth of the MBS Securitization monster that caused the mortgage meltdown and global financial crisis of 2008.

The aftermath of rampant foreclosures caused in this process still haunt and prey upon American citizens in the tens of millions.

Why didn't President Clinton veto the repeal of the Banking Act of 1933? He knew the premise upon which it was created. Clinton balanced the budget. Clinton understood America's finances and was a historian of America's past, just as many presidents are.

Some might argue that allowing an impeachment trial soured Clinton on Americans. Others might argue his establishment in 1997 of the

Nitty Gritty of MBS © 2016 Richard M. Kahn

Clinton Foundation needed funding and the bank lobby was one of the richest. Whatever the reason, it occurred.

President Bill Clinton opened the Pandora's box in that repeal. Massive foreclosures, unemployment, huge federal deficits incurred to avoid massive Depression that remain unparalleled in breadth across American history. America is now faced with some $20 Trillion in debt and growing because of it. The initial onslaught of the meltdown in 2008 actually began in the second half of 2007.

The Mortgage Meltdown of 2008 began with a run on some banks. This was handled quickly thanks to the FDIC depositor insurance protection and intervention. One of the first to experience the collapse and failure was monolithic Washington Mutual Bank on September 25, 2008. On this day the United States Office of Thrift Supervision ("OTS") banking regulators seized Washington Mutual Bank from Washington Mutual, Inc. ("WaMu") and placed it into the receivership of the Federal Deposit Insurance Corporation ("FDIC"). The OTS took this action due to the withdrawal of $16.4 billion in deposits, during a 10-day bank run. That was 9% of the deposits WaMu reportedly held just three months earlier on June 30, 2008. It was the biggest bank failure in American history to that date.

WaMu's failure was the first mega bank consolidation one of the handful of banks that would remain alive today garnered for a song. WaMu had over $300 billion in assets before it was shut down and the FDIC sold its assets to JPMorgan Chase for under $2 billion. This was reminiscent of Great Depression era windfalls by giant banks.

The Banking Act of 1933 established the Federal Deposit Insurance Corporation ("FDIC"). The FDIC insures deposits in banks and seizes banks in trouble. It can operate them until it sells them or assists in the mergers of failing banks with healthy ones. In this process the FDIC can take a sizable financial hit to their insurance fund. The FDIC is backed, like the entire federal government, by the American people's taxpayer base.

President Franklin D. Roosevelt ("FDR") was the only president to have been voted into office on four consecutive terms. FDR's presidency spanned from the Great Depression era in 1932 through the Second World War in mid 1945 when he died while in office. He became wheelchair bound after contracting polio in 1921 at age 29.

FDR's Administration created many important government regulatory agencies that have become bulwarks of consumer protections. Many of which relate to our specific subject matters and as a result, to our best defenses against wrongful foreclosure.

One such agency created was the Securities and Exchange Commission ("SEC"). The SEC regulates the public corporation and investment banking side of things. The SEC is still a critically important part of MBS securitization today. The SEC protects the public and requires entities offering securities to the public to openly file documentation and reporting with the SEC. These are sworn federal filings. Lies or deceit are punishable to the full extent of the law. The SEC played a critical role instigating the Mortgage Meltdown of 2008 and its aftermath. The SEC plays both a regulatory and policing role.

Birth of the MBS Securitization *monster* came with then president Bill Clinton's pen in November 1999. Birth of MBS Securitization that worked is attributed to the investment banking firm Salomon Brothers. In the mid to late 1970's they established a mortgage trading desk, the precursor to MBS . Fannie Mae originated their first collateralized mortgage obligations around 1983.MBS has been around. It became toxic with the repeal of the banking act that kept the greedy collusion of commercial mortgage bankers from going into cahoots with investment bankers. The birth date of toxic MBS Securitization coincided with New Years Eve 1999/2000.

On this day the Globe of countries and peoples feared their lives would collapse in every sector because computers could fail to properly handle date management. We called this specter "Y2K". Y2K was the media darling.

Y2K did not materialize as the disaster it was portended to be. Little media attention went to the parallel disaster that *did* materialize: The 106th Congress repealing the Banking Act of 1933 in November 1999 and outgoing President Clinton signing it into law just before he left office. No hoopla, no champagne. January 1, 2000,opened what proved to be a flood gate of predatory MBS Securitization. America and indeed the entire world would suffer the worst financial and economic crisis as a result.

Deregulation and MBS Securitization attracted American homeowners to predatory loans by the tens of millions. Investors purchased them in mortgage pools by the trillions of dollars.

There are those who might give a big thanks to President Bill Clinton for his part, but it is not the homeowner that lost or is faced with losing their home to wrongful foreclosure. It is not the institutions involved with MBS Securitizations that were wiped out and turned to ashes by the SEC for their role in the financial crisis.

Giving thanks are the handful of banks remaining that now control the majority or America's assets, along with the demise of thousands of bank competitors whose assets include those the big banks now own. It is the remaining servicing arms of the big lenders who are amassing millions of homes by foreclosure that they don't have a dime loaned out on. It is the major corporations that are now humongous conglomerates because they bought up strong companies when their stocks were cents on the dollar as a result of the financial crisis. It is the foreign countries like China, who loaned money to or waived collecting money due from America and now are our silent bankers sucking up much of America's annual GDP in interest due and glutting the market with cheap prices in every sector.

The allure of MBS Securitization appealed to America's homeowner greed in the guise of easy mortgage money that was widely available. No one cared about the details of whether loans were traditional "portfolio" mortgages where banks lent money to borrowers and serviced the loan as an investment; or MBS securitized loans they knew nothing about.

With repeal of the Banking Act of 1933 in November 1999, investors on a global level could pour trillions into buying American mortgage loans. Originating lenders transferred the risk of lending for payment in full, in cash, at or close to the time of loan origination. When it came time for default, the servicing arms of lenders swooped in and manipulate the court system if necessary in the quest to foreclose by any means before anyone was/is the wiser to what's really going on.

Two questions are often raised in the hallways of foreclosure courts. How do lenders who we thought were lending us money weren't? And not having lent us money, how are the lender's servicing arms winning homeowner's properties without ever loaning out any money and without actually representing investors who can actually prove they own the loans they seek to foreclose on?

One of the answers is the type of loan products American homeowners were duped into accepting. Loans destined to default.

In the Great Depression Era the aggressive loan products consisted of mainly "interest only balloon" mortgages. Borrowers would pay for several years only to find they owed the same amount as they did when they originally took the loans out. The catch was that several years down the road when the mortgages ballooned, there was not enough equity in the property to refinance. The mortgage was due and new replacement financing was not possible as no equity existed in the property. So the bank wound up seizing the property through foreclosure. They took the foreclosed property into their real estate owned ("REO") portfolios then resold them with new mortgage financing to another unsuspecting borrower. The fresh borrower walked in thinking they were getting the home of their dreams and a mortgage they could afford. Just like the original borrower thought. Soon the new buyers were out of a home in the same way as the old borrowers were and the new borrowers realized the mortgage was toxic. It was the opposite of a great deal. But it was too late.

We can find a parallel picture of the typical borrower in the Great Depression days and today. History records cartoons of the proverbial foreclosing banker in black hat and suit clutching a deed in one hand and a poor damsel in distress homeowner being foreclosed upon tied by rope on the railroad tracks. The foreclosure train barreling towards her from the distance. A familiar scenario today as then, without the top hat.

This cartoon image depicts the scary nightmare of reality for tens of millions American homeowners today.

Nitty Gritty of MBS © 2016 Richard M. Kahn

The exit strategy of banks in the Great Depression era that precipitated the institution of the Banking Act of 1933 is the same as the bank's exit strategy today. Gaining REO property by foreclosure, with one big difference. Today the banks and their servicing arms don't have a dime loaned out on that property. The mortgage loans were sold so many times and paid off so many times, they are often floating in the ether with no investor claiming ownership. So the Servicers fabricate wrongful foreclosure to win the property instead. Unlike the public and government regulators, the mortgage and investment bankers got smarter over the decades spanning The Great Depression. Beginning in 2000, mortgage bankers sold the mortgages to investment banker's investor clients for immediate profit, total release from financial risk and an agreement to service the loan at fees amounting to about $28 per month on each $100,000 of loan amount. Good business in bulk by the millions of loans to service as we'll see details of in the Mortgage Servicing Chapter 19.

A business made all the better with the prospect of capturing a percentage of defaulted loans for their own REO portfolios which they didn't loan money out on and didn't have to pay an owner off for on foreclosure. Creative accounting and owners who were paid off already insured that valuable prospect.

Unscrupulous default loan servicing in a deregulated environment is stealing American homeowner's homes.

Actual loan servicing includes running the day to day loan operations with the borrower. It puts the loan servicing branches of mortgage bankers smack dab in the driver's seat with default loan servicing operations. Timing, having a finger on the pulse of to foreclose when the time is right for them is a calibrated part of the process. It has a name, Default Loan Servicing.

Legally speaking, these loan servicers are just third party vendors. They are not true owners and State Laws exist for borrowers to capitalize on this in their fight against wrongful foreclosure. A troubling part of the equation for borrowers facing these actions is the caliber of attorney(s) representing the borrowers. Unfortunately most are not on their A game.

Many foreclosure attorneys faced with the geysers of foreclosures all of a sudden, decided to change their shingles from real estate closing and immigration attorneys to foreclosure attorneys.

Attorneys from both sides are thinking borrowers are deadbeats. The truth in MBS Securitization conducted from 2000 on is, loans have been sold so many times over for profits having been turned into commodities to do so. It begs the question, does a borrower still owe on that mortgage? Many borrower's position is they do not. They want a fair share for turning their home into a profit that enriched someone 8 times over, since they didn't know that was the deal in the first place. They want some disgorgement and restitution in the form of about 1/8th of the profits. A lot less than Uncle Sam takes in most tax scenarios providing much less for the individual. That's their argument. Of course opposing counsel sees it differently. The fight is going to boil down to can the person claiming ownership prove ownership. The issues are pretty simple. But explaining it and understanding it in terms of MBS Securitization to win over a judge is another story.

Litigating contested foreclosure is unlike closing a real estate deal. performing title work or filling out immigration forms. It is all about making a case in court that a Judge will examine facts and documentation considered for evidence. It is safe to say a large percentage of foreclosure attorneys don't truly litigate the case. They simply stall and move the case sideways. Borrower stays in the home and attorney gets monthly fees until the case is tried and lost.

It is infinitely more difficult to present and argue a case in court when you don't have a clue to all the ins and outs behind the party's claiming ownership. Copy pasting pleading arguments from the Internet and throwing it out hoping it will stick and win is mostly a pipe dream. Judges want to understand everything that pertains to equitable fairness in a decision.

The servicing lenders have nothing to lose if a borrower's case goes against them in court and the loan servicer is not able to foreclose. They simply set that one case to the side and move on to the next one. It's a matter of numbers. The fact loan servicers are brazen enough to lie, falsify documents, misrepresent ownership and commit intrinsic and extrinsic fraud on the court in the process.

Blatant fraud upon courts is a commonality as one of the first actions of taking over a country. Many third world countries experience this mocking of their courts. As such it is very important to expose the truth and the lies to protect the integrity of the courts in America.

Chapter 2

Turning mortgages into commodities for staggering profits

A good question becomes, how did the participants in MBS Securitization turn $1 of mortgage into $8 of profit? The answer is, MBS Securities turned mortgages into a commodity that could trade in their own marketplace like futures do. By way of analogy, it didn't matter one hog that cost $1 traded for $8. It was supply and demand.

In January 2000 the repeal of the Banking Act of 1933 enabled the commercial and investment banks to join forces again. They were unable to do so since taking part in orchestrating the Great Depression. Now they needed vehicles to ply their trade.

One key to that process offering many individual products and a marketplace was created by the Commodity Futures Modernization Act of 2000. ("CFMA 2000")

The CFMA 2000 amended the Banking Act of 1933 (a/k/a the Gramm-Leach-Bliley Act). It also amended the Securities and Exchange Act of 1932 and the Securities Act of 1933 and set a marketplace in the Over the Counter ("OTC") market for trading mortgage backed securities, ("MBS") "derivatives" and "swaps". Congress passed this act in a period of days from its introduction. President Bill Clinton did not veto this act, nor did he veto the repeal of the Banking Act of 1933.

Between 2000 and 2008, the banks and financial institutions across the Globe were trading some $62 Trillion dollars worth of these MBS derivatives. Corporations, Governments, Investors and other Institutions carried these as assets on their balance sheets.

That wouldn't be a problem except that there were only some $8 trillion of real underlying mortgages secured by actual unique underlying real properties backing them up! The commodities nature of MBS Securitization enabled this result.

Fannie Mae and Freddie Mac, the Government Sponsored Enterprises ("GSEs") established to facilitate lending in America only accounted for some $5 trillion dollars of real underlying mortgages. Private Label MBS claimed to have accounted for some $3 trillion in real underlying mortgages on real properties.

Inflating the value of these $8 trillion in actual properties and actual mortgages created a National Security risk to America as well as a portent of danger to American homeowners, borrowers who took out mortgages during the years 2000 through 2008. It also put the global economy at risk.

Let's look at what the number $62 Trillion represents. That will give an initial idea of the problem. $62 Trillion equals all the product created in one year by all the billions of people in all of the countries on the face of planet Earth.

Obviously, selling supply and demand based assets of mortgage loans in MBS Securitizations equal to the entire gross world product was a windfall of profit. Calculated from both the selling price of the products themselves that didn't' exist and fees on those products that didn't exist. In our hog analogy, only the one hog existed, the 8 others sold did not exist, it was trading value of a commodity future.

Grave National Security concerns arose in the process. The SEC and other federally regulated corporations, banks, financial institutions as well as government, were carrying highly inflated assets on their books as real assets. These assets became a basis upon which financial markets relied to assess the value of these entities and their total worth of holdings. These falsely inflated valuations attracted investors to stocks of companies and caused an unprecedented rise in stock prices. Financial markets were now being driven by falsities in accounting and valuation.

Before we look at why this occurrence caused the SEC and Federal Accounting Standards Board ("FASB") to shut the whole thing down by collapsing the financial markets which destroyed thousands of banking institutions that took part in it. The lucky few remaining experienced the same conglomerate building and banking consolidation which echoed those that took place in the Great Depression days as well,

Let's explore the mechanics of creating mortgages as commodities, to trade on the value pegged by investor demand and not reflective of underlying individual mortgages. In other words the $8x of value on the $1 of actual underlying mortgage. This is the foundation of creating MBS securitization

People may think of commodities as agricultural products and raw materials. Sugar, salt, corn, pork bellies, wheat, rice, et cetera, are agricultural materials. Aluminum, copper, silver, platinum, silicon et cetera, are raw materials. Petroleum, crude oil, coal, natural gas, et cetera, are energy commodities.

The concept is based on actual "delivery". Commodities include "futures". Futures are a commodities business *bet*. If you do not own the product at the time or you may not produce enough to cover your unfilled sales orders or anticipated product needs, you can cover your *future* needs by buying or insuring against unforeseen product needs in the "future".

Trading in commodities futures can also gamble on making profits in the interim, depending on how they perceive the price and availability to move values on the underlying commodity during the term of time remaining on their futures contracts.

For example, trading for profits may find an investor buying barrels of oil at $x with no intention of actually taking delivery. The intention is to trade on the anticipated value of oil before delivery.

Nitty Gritty of MBS © 2016 Richard M. Kahn

This is the scenario MBS Securitization finds itself in, investors and securitization parties trading for profits before delivery.

Creating commodities on "stocks" came into existence in 1973 with the establishment of the Chicago Board of Options Exchange (CBOE), founded to trade options and futures. The author was one of the first to be licensed to trade commodities on the CBOE. The vehicles were called Options, comprised of puts, calls and hedges. Congress must have understood Options in 2000 when the Commodity Futures Modernization Act of 2000 was passed. That would explain why the Act only needed about one week to pass.

With its passage, commercial and investment banks were free to create a commodities market on pooled mortgage assets in "Mortgage Backed Securities" (MBS). Trading these MBS "derivatives" on the Over the Counter (OTC) market the transactions did not report as trades do on exchanges such as the NYSE, AMEX and other highly regulated trading markets.

By utilizing the Over The Counter (OTC) virtual marketplace, commercial and investment banks avoided the restrictions of listed marketplaces. Products, contract specifications and limited maturities already existed on the Chicago Board Options Exchange (CBOE) and OneExchange. Trades could be tracked.

In the OTC marketplace, regulators could easily be kept in the dark. Commercial and investment banks made up the foundation of the derivatives market. Banking and Securities regulators found themselves relying on "self-regulation". The derivatives desks in the trading rooms of these institutions could hide information.

The OTC market provided a platform where an infinite number of derivative contract specifications, underlying assets, maturities and modified terms could exist as long as there were clients, counterparties and investors across the global markets who were willing to deal.

With a minimum of two parties, a derivative can be created out of anything. For example: currencies, commodities, stocks, interest rates, bonds, et cetera. You could own the underlying asset or not, it was up to the terms of your contract. You could be trading for cash or futures. Basically, as long as there was someone else out there willing to make a contract and trade, you could create a derivative investment vehicle tailored to the agreement of terms between the parties.

Credit Default Swaps (CDS) were an especially ingenious derivative investment idea. CDS were designed to transfer the risk of default on the underlying mortgages in the mortgage backed security to the seller of the CDS. Investors clamored to reduce their risk in the underlying mortgage pools. They agreed to pay fees in the process.

The buyers (investors purchasing certificates in the underlying mortgage pools) could buy insurance guaranteeing the credit worthiness of the borrowers and insuring mortgage holders against default in the mortgage payments and or the mortgages themselves; even the lowering of the credit rating placed on the underlying mortgages themselves.

The seller of the CDS assumes the risk in exchange for fees and is only required to pay out in case the negative action (default, downgraded credit, et cetera) occurs. A great concept that was rooted in principal from the Great Depression days The Federal Housing Administration ("FHA") began insuring loans for small fees in 1934. The FHA is part of the U.S. Housing and Urban Development ("HUD").

FHA single family programs require and upfront fee called a Mortgage Insurance Premium ("MIP"). Leading up to the year 2000, FHA's public financial records evidence the Mortgage Insurance Premiums far exceed actual defaults in underlying mortgages. It looked like a profitable enterprise. As a result of the financial crisis, that has changed drastically and FHA could be the next bailout candidate. More on that in Chapter 12.

A critical enabler of CDS contracts selling for $8x on only $1x of actual underlying mortgage is that CDS only need to *reference* the underlying assets. CDS do not need to "own" or control the underlying asset.

Given these parameters, the mortgage and investment banks brought a wide and complex array of derivatives into the marketplace. The Over The Counter (OTC) trading platform that enabled any derivative to trade as long as there were at least two parties willing to trade it, was a perfect globally accessible virtual setting. Trading desks anywhere in the world could trade instantly on the OTC. In the unregulated OTC marketplace "anything went".

Leverage was inherent to the derivatives themselves to multiply gains and losses. For example, one could leverage twenty million worth of mortgage backed securities with one million of cash. This is commonly referred to as buying or selling on "margin".

Traders created contracts to bet on every aspect they could think of and find a willing party to buy. The market spiraled out of control. The CDS derivatives became less about conservative "insurance" and all about speculative trading profits.

Traders were putting contracts on every conceivable aspect of the underlying asset. Betting against the asset defaulting, betting against the seller collecting payments, betting against the fees being sufficient to cover potential losses, betting against maturity exposures, betting against lowering of credit ratings. Anything went as long as a minimum of two parties agreed to it.

Getting to $62 *trillion* dollars in total commodity asset value on $8 trillion dollars in actual real unique underlying properties securing the mortgages, required diluting the underlying mortgage security interests. On delivery there was only $1x of mortgage underlying the trade. Those trading it up to $8x made or lost money on bets along the way prior to delivery, which in MBS mortgage backed securities finds underlying assets amortizing over long maturity years. Most often 20-40 years on mortgages. Plenty of time to trade before delivery or satisfaction of the underlying debt took a mortgage out of a pool. Refinances, foreclosures and the like could shortened those times from a practical sense. Still it was years. A long time to allow for trading. MBS derivatives in our case began in 2000 and didn't reach their pinnacle of value until 2007 or so.

Smart people plan a strategy that will keep them out of jail. The problem was how to accomplish that without misrepresenting the actual investment itself. The Securities and Exchange Commission ("SEC") investigates and arrests people who misrepresent products and defraud the public.

To solve this problem of a dramatic shortage of real property underlying mortgages in pools, several products were created. One of them enabled buyers to buy excess cash flows from mortgages. Another enabled them to buy certificates of previously issued mortgage backed securities. The epitome of smoke and mirrors was the creation of Synthetic CDS (Credit Default Swaps) contracts.

Now the portfolio of assets behind the trading vehicle need not exist at all. The Synthetic was set up to "imitate" portfolios of assets such as the mortgage backed securities (MBS) of the same credit risk and potential default payoff aspects that might be considered.

The high and mighty trading departments that participated in this process and transacting trillions of dollars, were just desks. Traders

Nitty Gritty of MBS © 2016 Richard M. Kahn

and departments earned astronomical amounts of commissions and fees for themselves and their financial institutions. Brokers with a desk, computer terminals and phones. Earning commissions on transacting nearly $8 trillion a year from averaged out on the total $62 trillion transacted between 2000 through 2007.

Account executives manning trading desks are not considered analysts, they are sales people. They may learn enough about a product to trade them, but in general they are thought to rarely examine the underlying assets themselves. It is rare to find commodities traders examining pig pens or the bellies of oil tankers to confirm the actual products. The same is true with MBS mortgage assets. They were interested in commissions and fees.

Investors of all types felt they had plenty of years before the underlying CDS would mature. They freely held them in assets on their balance sheets, accumulating them in vast quantities.

This is one reason many loan modifications are not made. Modifying the loan would alter the derivatives swap contracts. A complex renegotiation whose principals were not interested in doing so. They understood refinances or foreclosures taking out underlying properties but loan modifications created different terms and could

Nitty Gritty of MBS © 2016 Richard M. Kahn

mean renegotiating the entire CDS. This was the commodities factor. There was another factor that prevented loan mods as well. We'll cover that in Chapter 17, Credit Enhancement. Briefly, in the MBS Securitization different groups of certificate holders that were insured by loans in other groups (Subordination) would be harmed by loan mods as well.

To spice up the earnings, savvy market makers in MBS derivatives made money, even when they were losing money. The purchaser of a derivative contract can sell to a willing buyer and make a profit in a number of ways.

They could be "long", making money betting the price would go up; buying low and selling high.

They could sell "short", making money if the price went down; borrowing and selling high then buying low to cover and returning the contract minus the profits.

They could hedge or "offset" using another contract with another party, making money trading inside or outside of a price value range.

Not only price values could be hedged. Actual terms underlying the CDS could be hedged. For example, interest rate hedges.

One didn't need a depth of knowledge of the underlying asset, they just needed to make money in the trade. The key element in the derivatives was leverage.

Fact checking the $8 trillion and $62 trillion numbers used. Several years prior to the financial collapse and Mortgage Meltdown of 2008, the International Swaps and Derivatives Association ("ISDA") reported in 2007 that Credit Default Swaps worldwide were some $62 *trillion* and all swaps worldwide totaled over five *hundred trillion*. Yet, only *some $8* trillion of actual mortgages securing this.

Chapter 3

Traditional Lending vs. MBS "mortgages in certificates out" lending

Now that the commodities aspect of mortgage loans has been covered, let's take a look at what MBS securitization does to mortgage loan assets, enabling them to be sold over and over and over again. Notes are the I.O.U., mortgages are the security. In this book, the term "Mortgage" can also mean "Deed of Trust".

Traditional Loan

In a traditional portfolio mortgage loan, bank's evaluated borrowers based upon the bank's underwriting criteria. Savings banks and commercial banks had depositor's money and making prudent loans to borrowers who had demonstrated income and financial stability on real property with strong appraisals was good business.

Interest rates on loans with strong underlying property that had equity in them provided better rates of return on investments than other investment vehicles like municipal bonds, corporate bonds and U.S. Treasury securities.

The property underlying the loan was evaluated and appraised. The borrower's income and ability to repay was examined closely. Foreclosure was a last resort which could cost the bank money.

At the loan closing with the borrower, the bank received the initial original Note which was the promise to pay and the Mortgage, which represented the security interest of the property. These two documents together were like gold. The bank exercised considerable caution in handling these documents, especially the Note. They put the Note into the vault, sent the mortgage out for recording in the county records right away and then reunited the properly recorded Mortgage with the Note. Often simply placed, inside a manila folder.

The loan was then serviced in terms of day to day administration with the borrower as a long term investment.

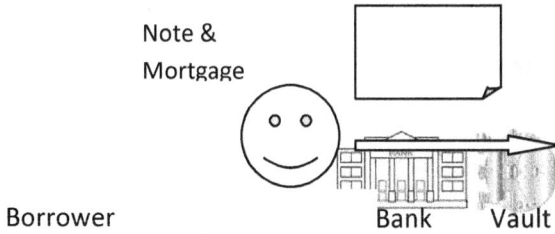

Note & Mortgage

Borrower   Bank   Vault

The initial original Note and Mortgage that the borrower signed were together and safely secured in the bank's vault. These initial originals are what we commonly call "the blue ink wet signed originals".

Mortgage Backed Securities (MBS) Lending

In MBS securitization mortgage loans go in and certificates resembling stock certificates or bond certificates come out. Investors buy the certificates and trade the certificates. The price of a certificate is based on supply and demand, so it seeks its own value. The more secure the certificate investment seems to be, the more value it has to an investor. These investors are trading certificates. They are not in the origination of commodities business. They are not pumping oil, raising hogs, herding cattle or originating or servicing mortgages.

MBS securitizations are large size transactions, Typically in the several hundreds of millions of dollars and often over one billion dollars of initial mortgage loan assets per deal. Somewhere in the MBS marketplace deals were coming out and selling out every day from 2000 to 2007.

In 2000, mortgage backed securitization basically did away with traditional mortgage lending. Now if mortgages were originated for portfolio they were held for sale to MBS securitizations.

Mortgage bankers and Wall Street investment bankers got together and financially engineered a new breed of mortgages and securities through the innovative design of packaging mortgages into huge billion dollar collections called "mortgage pools". These pools would then be sold to investors by Wall Street investment banks.

Residential and commercial properties could be securitized in this way. Residential pools typically represented more loans of smaller size than commercial loans. Some residential loans called "jumbos" on homes of high value were pooled together.

Mortgage backed securitizations could run into the $1 billion to $1.5 billion dollar range and represent 4,000 to 5,000 separate loans, each evidenced by a Note which represented the borrower's I.O.U., and a

Nitty Gritty of MBS © 2016 Richard M. Kahn

Mortgage (or Deed of Trust) which represented the security interest in the property.

Securitization is the process of taking illiquid assets, in this case individual mortgages, and placing them into a "mortgage pool". This involves a series of independent "true sales" and financial engineering   by a number of different parties in order to transform the pooled mortgages into a security owned by investors and represented by a Trustee.

These "true sales" are at the heart of the securitization to ensure the investors have the unequivocal legal right of ownership, without doubt, to the mortgage assets and receivables in the trust.

Through the "true sales" process the investors' ownership is protected from potential bankruptcy or claims made against the originating lender or interim owners of the mortgage(s). Sales of the securitized assets develop their own value in the marketplace, depending on various factors. Such as prevailing interest rates at the time. Resales of the same mortgage over and over dilute the asset owned. It may be sold for $8x but it is still only secured by $1x of actual mortgage. In that scenario the asset is split 8 ways instead of one. These shares or bonds may be split or resold or included in other

Nitty Gritty of MBS © 2016 Richard M. Kahn

assets sold. For this reason, the Notes and Mortgages are no longer individually attached to the specific asset because they aren't attached to whole loans.

This financial engineering begins when the mortgages in the pool are grouped into classes based upon mortgage type and borrower credit. The credit of these classes is then enhanced and rated by credit ratings agencies such as S&P and Moody's. These credit enhanced mortgages are repackaged and then sold to investors. The investors then typically purchase insurance in case of mortgage default.

 Investors evidence their ownership in the mortgages through certificates (notes), or debt agreements (bonds), or rights to ownership (derivatives) similar to stocks and bonds.

The securitization legal documentation establishes asset acquisition and loan servicing authority by agreements. It establishes a method of proving ownership in the traditional sense by describing the endorsements we should expect to find on the Note and identify the Document Custodian who holds these originals. All these documents are considered sworn oath federal filings when they are submitted to the Securities and Exchange Commission under Regulation AB rules of disclosure designed to protect consumers.

Chapter 4

Evaluating Ponzi Characteristics of the Mortgage Crisis

We are going to see in the next chapter that the SEC took drastic actions against the MBS Securitization industry as it spiraled upwards in values of MBS derivatives held as assets on the accounting books. Let's look at some of the common characteristics of that may have prompted "red flag" warning signs.

Borrower's credit in loan origination of mortgages in the pools. Creditworthiness of borrowers in the lending industry were generally based on a model created by the Fair, Isaac and Company (FICO: NYSE) , known as "FICO" scores. When a borrower applied for credit the credit issuer could evaluate and measure the risk of the borrower defaulting on payments.

Three major Credit Bureaus kept track of consumer credit in the United States and reported the scores to creditors and lenders inquiring. These were Equifax, Experian and TransUnion. When a borrower made application and gave their permission, the creditor would "pull" the consumers' credit scores.

The credit history models looked at payment history over time. It kept track of late payments or timely payments in any given month. It tracked negative reporting items such as late payments, foreclosures, repossessions, charge offs, judgments and judgment liens and filings such as bankruptcy.

FICO scores also looked at the burden of debt on a consumer's credit. How many accounts they had, what the balances were against the limits, the type of accounts, how often and how much they paid down on revolving and installment loans.

Creditors chose whether they wanted to pull all three, or pull only specific Credit Bureau scores when a consumer applied for a loan or a line of credit from a card issuer.

FICO scores changed over time. During the period of mortgage lending we are addressing the range of FICO scores on borrowers applying for mortgages were generally considered in the 550 to 770 range. The range of score a borrower was in affected their lending class of mortgage borrower. For example: Sub-prime below 620. Prime, 720 and above.

The borrower's credit score determined the interest rate they would pay on their mortgage loan and other credit loans. The higher the score, the lower the interest rate.

Masking Risk to Investors buying MBS Securities

MBS Securitizations promised investors very highly rated securities. Sponsors of MBS Securitization would arrange Credit Enhancements on pools of mortgages that purported to raise the underlying borrower debt up to AAA, the highest investment grade ratings issued. AAA ratings normally reserved for such secure entities as the strongest public companies, utilities, municipalities and government issuances.

Various methods of credit enhancement, which are detailed in Chapter 17, were presented to the Ratings Agencies such as Moody's, S&P and Fitch. With the highest AAA ratings attached, investors accepted lower interest rates on their investments, typical of very highly secured underlying debt repayment quality security.

Representations in offering prospectuses on MBS Securitizations touted these Credit Enhancements and insurance guarantees in such a way that the Ratings Agencies believed the underlying model was extremely secure. That was dominated in part with a representation that defaults in underlying mortgages would be in the fractional percentages. In fact, underlying mortgages eventually began to default in massive amounts representing high percentages of the underlying mortgage pool assets.

Investors in MBS Securitizations and the Ratings Agencies rating them weren't as suspicious of these, little or no risk representations.

The MBS Securitizations promised overly consistent returns to investors, basing these projections on Credit Enhancements and Insurances (detailed in Chapter 17), that proved far too little to prop up the MBS mortgage pools enough to maintain the high investment grade credit ratings. These promises were false and misleading.

The underlying loan origination strategies were secretive and complex. Loan origination, represents the basis of the mortgage assets. Investors saw Ratings of AAA. Loan originators and parties selling the mortgage loans in the process to the MBS Securitization Trusts made representations and warranties against default of the underlying individual mortgages. These promised to substitute or buy back loans that went into early default or were defective in securing the Notes and Mortgages. These promises were on top of the Credit Enhancement promises.

These promises fell flat and did nothing to account for the lowering of underwriting standards in loan origination that prevailed. Mortgage bankers and lenders needed to generate mortgage loans in vast quantities to meet the extraordinary demand created by the investment bankers pushing their investors into the MBS Securitizations. MBS securitizations were coming out weekly with average deal sizes in the hundreds of millions and often billions.

To attract borrowers in unprecedented numbers Originators began offering low teaser interest rates that would adjust but for the initial fixed periods promised big savings to borrowers over existing interest payments and caused many to refinance. Oftentimes these refinances included "cash out" to the borrower, stimulating reasons to refinance as well.

To attract even more borrowers, the mortgage bankers and lenders lowered the creditworthiness requirements borrowers needed to meet to obtain mortgage financing. In the process, attracting trillions of dollars of sub-prime borrowers to make mortgage loans they would eventually default on. With such caveats as no income, no asset loan underwriting standards anyone could get financing.

The representations and warranties by the mortgage banks and lenders to repurchase and buy back these loans at the amounts they sold these loans to the investors, present in nearly every MBS Securitization deal's agreements, were false and misleading.

The bank Trustee's who managed the MBS Securitizations were most often affiliated or participating in the MBS Securitization process. Investors took the promises on face value. They did not look deeply into the underlying asset security.

An additional impediment to the complexities of the loan origination issues were the interim sale and securitization activities of the intervening SPE bankruptcy remote ownership transition where the "magic" of mortgages in, certificate securities out took place. This will be detailed in Private Label Securitization Chapter 7.

Investors in MBS Securitization did not avoid making investments employing these secretive techniques and processes in formation and intervening sales. The activities in these areas by the participants did not offer detailed information. They remain so complex today that many do not understand them. This book demystifies these complexities in layman's terms.

In hindsight investors should have avoided making investments in products they did not fully understand and did not have enough information to truly decipher and analyze the underlying investment. They simply took their account executive's word at the MBS Securities trading desk.

Investors did not become suspicious that the MBS Securitizations promised to generate regular positive returns over time, no matter what the overall market conditions did. The MBS Securities were originated and offered to investors in a period of rising real estate values, fueled by easy mortgage money. Near the end it seemed like everyone in America could become a homeowner and a real estate investor.

Much of the underlying mortgage financing required increasing home values to sustain. When the record home prices leveled off, borrowers were not able to exit their mortgages by selling the properties for profits. And as interest rates on the underlying mortgages began to adjust those borrowers could not meet the payments. Loans began to default, home prices began to come down. This began to escalate, causing a great deal of defaults.

Investors were not suspect that the consistent returns they were promised and the representations and warranties by the originators to repurchase defaulting loans as overall market conditions worsened, would not protect their investments.

Investors bought into the no legitimate earnings scheme.
Using our example of $1 in underlying mortgage on real property being sold up to $8x times. The only real cash flow that underlay the transaction was a simple mortgage payment. MBS derivative, sales, re-sales and MBS re-issuances of already issued MBS began mount up and drive the values of the $1x up on its way up to the eventual $8x before the collapse,

Investors did not realize there were no other legitimate earnings to pay the interest returns on those $2x to $8x investments. The underlying mortgage only covered the $1x. What paid the interest on the $2x to $8x investments was only the consistent cash flow of money from new investors continuing to purchase.

Shoddy mortgage origination paperwork was ignored.
Any attorney or Trustee representing a buyer in a simple real estate mortgage purchase would be provided the loan origination documentation at a simple closing, *then* fund the purchase.

The relevant information was "trusted" the be reviewed by parties to the MBS Securitization but in fact was not. The MBS Trustees and Investors broke the cardinal rule of real estate mortgage lending. Only fund the mortgage purchase after all the documentation and recordings are performed. Never do so before.

Chains of title and ownership were secretive and complex.
The bankruptcy remote aspects of mortgages in and certificate securities out were complex and secretive. The actions of the intervening SPE model were not required to consolidate assets and liabilities and report them on their quarterly or annual reports. (Detailed in SPE Bank Securitization Chapter 14).

MERS was created by the banks together to bypass proper recording. This scheme has singlehandedly defrauded millions of homeowners via wrongful foreclosure and caused them to lose homes. Investors also lost because many of these foreclosures were stripped from inuring to the investor's benefits. Instead foreclosure properties with to servicer's Real Estate Owned IREO) portfolios and the act of foreclosure stripped the investors of being able to go after the loan servicers. See MERS - Tool of Deception, Chapter 16.

This lack of confirming and being able to confirm simple mortgage transaction purchases was a clear sign that the investment that investors were paying for were not purchasing mortgage loans in the responsible manner they were promised to have been purchased.

The collapse came when new investor investments dried up.
When the consistent cash flow of new investor money dried up, the money needed to pay on the to pay off on the $2x to $8x interest payments dried up.

One of the logical explanations we have as to why the SEC brought the whole house down in such speedy fashion of nearly overnight, is that the issues of fact presented are all "red flags" the SEC defines as those of a "Ponzi Scheme".

The SEC publishes these on their web site, which at the time of this writing is located online at: http://www.sec.gov/answers/ponzi.htm

For the convenience of the reader, here are a few excerpts in pertinent part, quoted from the SEC's publication: U.S. Securities and Exchange Commission's (SEC) *"Ponzi Schemes – Frequently Asked Questions"*.[1]

"The SEC investigates and prosecutes many Ponzi scheme cases each year both to prevent new victims from being harmed and to maximize the recovery of assets to investors. The majority of such cases are brought as emergency actions, which often seek a temporary restraining order and an asset freeze. "

"What is a Ponzi scheme?
A Ponzi scheme is an investment fraud that involves the payment of purported returns to existing investors from funds contributed by new investors. Ponzi scheme organizers often solicit new investors by promising to invest funds in opportunities claimed to generate high returns with little or no risk. In many Ponzi schemes, the fraudsters focus on attracting new money to make promised payments to

---

[1] http://www.sec.gov/answers/ponzi.htm

45 | P a g e   Nitty Gritty of MBS © 2016 Richard M. Kahn earlier-stage investors and to use for personal expenses, instead of engaging in any legitimate investment activity."

"Why do Ponzi schemes collapse?
With little or no legitimate earnings, the schemes require a consistent flow of money from new investors to continue. Ponzi schemes tend to collapse when it becomes difficult to recruit new investors or when a large number of investors ask to cash out."

"Does the SEC investigate Ponzi schemes?
The SEC investigates and prosecutes many Ponzi scheme cases each year both to prevent new victims from being harmed and to maximize the recovery of assets to investors. The majority of such cases are brought as emergency actions, which often seek a temporary restraining order and an asset freeze. "

What are some Ponzi scheme "red flags"?
Many Ponzi schemes share common characteristics. Look for these warning signs:

> **High investment returns with little or no risk.** Every investment carries some degree of risk, and investments yielding higher returns typically involve more risk. Be highly suspicious of any "guaranteed" investment opportunity.

Overly consistent returns. Investments tend to go up and down over time, especially those seeking high returns. Be suspect of an investment that continues to generate regular, positive returns regardless of overall market conditions.

Secretive and/or complex strategies. Avoiding investments you don't understand or for which you can't get complete information is a good rule of thumb.

Issues with paperwork. Ignore excuses regarding why you can't review information about an investment in writing, and always read an investment's prospectus or disclosure statement carefully before you invest. Also, account statement errors may be a sign that funds are not being invested as promised.

Difficulty receiving payments. Be suspicious if you don't receive a payment or have difficulty cashing out your investment. Keep in mind that Ponzi scheme promoters sometimes encourage participants to "roll over" promised payments by offering even higher investment returns.

There is a disclaimer on this SEC page:

"We have provided this information as a service to investors. It is neither a legal interpretation nor a statement of SEC policy. If you have questions concerning the meaning or application of a particular law or rule, please consult with your attorney who specializes in securities law."

If this was indeed the biggest Ponzi scheme in history, it involved too many participants to start arresting and litigating. The SEC had to do something drastic, beyond anything it had ever done but within its power to do so. And that is exactly what they did.

Chapter 5

U.S. Government pulled the plug that caused financial collapse in 2008

We have just outlined in detail how commercial, mortgage and investment bankers created and exploited many tens of millions of homeowners with mortgages destined to default. These mortgages turned into commodities defrauded investors and had to be stopped, fast. Selling $1x of mortgages secured by single properties nearly $8x over, falsely inflated assets on balance sheets worldwide. The prevalence grew to a magnitude that threatened world economies and U.S. National Security. It had to be stopped and the perpetrators held accountable. This was accomplished nearly overnight, in emergency fashion.

We know the why from last chapter. This is the how.

Two U.S. Government agencies each made one simple change in financial regulation that caused the financial crisis of 2008, destroying banks and companies that perpetrated the fraud. Corporations, institutions, governments, pension funds, and investors were all holding MBS Securitization assets on their books that falsely boosted earnings, net worth and assets. Toxic MBS Securitizations were the basis of a false and ailing house of cards in this respect. It had to be rectified.

As far as policing, protracted litigation was not a choice. Too many huge powerful banks and lenders were involved. They could wage a long drawn out legal fight. The Securities and Exchange Commission ("SEC") acted swiftly and deliberately to permanently if not savagely, destroy corporation and bank participants that colluded to securitize private label MBS. It was an unprecedented bold move that had not been done in this magnitude, since the SEC was endowed to do so when they were created in the wake of the Great Depression.

Huge banking corporations, lenders and investment bankers found their entire corporations dissolved. This was justice of the boldest manner.

Nitty Gritty of MBS © 2016 Richard M. Kahn

Yes, some corporations whose executives were caught in frauds such as Taylor Bean & Whitaker and Colonial Bank were tried, found guilty and sentenced to long prison terms. But this is the exception, not the rule. Most banks and corporations in the private label MBS securitization industry were simply extinguished, wiped off the corporate map and did not rise from the ashes.

Three simple policy changes made by 2 agencies caused the financial collapse to occur overnight in days.

- Policy change 1 was the SEC causing the Federal Accounting Standards Board("FASB") to change the accounting rules to "mark to market".
- Policy change 2 was the SEC removing the stock exchanges "up-tick rule" that provided support to collapsing financial markets.

The result was a barn fire that roasted most participants involved with the MBS Securitization scandal. Two small changes that collapsed the financial markets, plunged participating financial institutions into non-existence and catapulted millions of Americans into foreclosure. In an exemplary way, proving the old adage "the pen is mightier than the sword".

Policy Change 1:

Accounting Change by the FASB to "mark to market".

The Federal Accounting Standards Board or "FASB" is the designated private sector organization in America that establishes financial accounting and reporting standards. The FASB issues accounting standards adopted by the U.S. Securities and Exchange Commission (SEC) as policy for publically traded institutions.

The FASB issued guidance change in September 2007. Financial institutions must change the manner in which they value their MBS securitization derivatives on their books.

Before the change, corporations and financial institutions valued their derivatives at maturity value. The asset was carried at its maturity value. If the asset had a face value of $1 million it was carried at that price on the books.

Mark to Market is the value a will buyer and seller will actually pay for that particular asset on a particular day. As we've learned, the MBS Securitizations in after trading were traded in the form of Derivatives, agreements between two parties that occurred privately in the Over the Counter markets.

On November 16, 2007, one month after the instruction to change the accounting method, we received our answer. The day after this FASB FAS 157 Mark to Market initiative became effective,

Financial markets began to collapse led by falling stock values of banks, financial institutions and corporations as their large positions in MBS Securitizations and MBS derivatives began to devalue overnight.

The plummet of stock values began with the Banks.

Banks are required to maintain certain Capital Ratios. The FDIC publishes White Papers on this topic. They insure depositors in bank failures. U.S. Banks regulated Capital Ratios came into existence in 1981, the year Donald Regan, CEO of Merrill Lynch became the U.S. Treasury Secretary under President Ronald Reagan. International banks followed in 1988 under the Basel Accord. The Capital ratios measure risk, leverage and gross revenue. Of all three, the risk weighted ratio is the strongest indicator of long term financial health.

Banks are required to comply with Capital Adequacy Ratios ("CARs") set by Federal and State banking regulators. The computation of CARs is quite complicated and involves different tiers of disclosed and

Nitty Gritty of MBS © 2016 Richard M. Kahn

undisclosed assets against liabilities and risk. Acceptable CARs insured Regulators the banks could absorb reasonable amounts of losses. At certain unacceptable levels bank stocks are forced to stop trading and at others the banks were closed by regulators.

Mark to Market pegged values on MBS and Derivatives to what a willing buyer would pay for that asset on the given day, not the face value of the asset.

The simple Present Value Calculation.

The SEC and FASB knew how to use Present Value calculations. It's a basic formula every financial advisor learns in the basics.

This present value of future assets is calculated using present value formulas that required 3 inputs. Face amount in the future, number of years to maturity and discount rate.

Discount Rate is the rate that the Fed lends money to its member banks. The historical rates are published on the Federal Reserve Bank's web site. In October 2007 the rate prior to the Mark to Market action, the Discount Rate was 5%.

Nitty Gritty of MBS © 2016 Richard M. Kahn

Using the calculator. Each $1 million of future value maturing in 30 years at a 5% discount rate was worth $231,000.

Calculating Capital Ratio a bank has to maintain
Using Tier 1 capital (for simplicity sake) regulators such as The Office of the Comptroller of the Currency determine if a bank is properly capitalized. Let's say the Capital Ratio requirement is 6%.

Let's use an example of how a bank's assets can Capital Ratio look the day before Mark to Market. We'll use a bank example with a combined shareholders equity and retained earning assets reporting of $10 million. This bank has risks weighted against those assets of $100 million. This is a Cap Ratio of 10%, far in excess of the minimum Capital Ratio requirement 6%.

Let's look at the bank's capital ratio the day after Mark to Market. Our discount calculation above at 5% discount rate reveals the new value of the assets is not $100 million, it's $23 million. ($10/$23 = 0.043). The Cap Ratio is 4.3%.

The bank is immediately at risk of halted trading or closure. The bank has to immediately sell liquid assets to cover. In our example the bank has to immediately raise its assets to $60 million.

To do this with the new valuation it has to theoretically sell $160 million of pre Mark to Mark assets which in our example is the day before Mark to Market set in, to obtain the $37 million it needs to boost its assets to $60 million ($37mm/.23)

Traders see assets plummeting and hold back from buying
Savvy Traders see prices on MBS and Derivatives plummeting overnight, they don't rush in to buy. They want to wait until prices hit support levels so they don't buy at prices which will go lower and insure losses.

This causes banks to panic
Maintaining regulatory Cap Ratios is a must, the shortfalls have to be covered immediately.

The banks try to raise cash by issuing Margin calls.

Understanding Margin and Leverage
Banks let customers owning marginable securities borrow against them. The customers can use the money for anything including buying more securities. This is called using "leverage".

Not all securities are marginable. A sizable number of listed stocks and bonds are marginable. It' up to the investment bank to decide on what is marginable for them.

Here is an example of securities that may be marginable.
Most of the stocks and ETSs (Exchange Traded Funds) traded on major exchanges (NYSE, AMEX, NASDAQ) with share prices over $3 are marginable. Mutual funds shares owned over 30 days. Most corporate bonds that are investment grade (includes MBS Securitizations) along with government bonds (municipals, agency and Treasury's).

Example of buying securities on Margin
Let' say the margin rate is 50% for ease of calculation. You are buying $10,000 worth of securities so you put up $5,000 and the investment bank acting as your broker lends you $5,000. Buying securities to earn money from a rise in price is called going "long".

Margin requirements are different for those investors who go "short" borrowing securities from their investment bank broker to sell and then hoping to buy them back cheaper in the future for a profit and returning the securities to the investment bank to cover their borrowing them in the first place. Margin for "short" selling using our

Nitty Gritty of MBS © 2016 Richard M. Kahn

example above is the value of the security transaction PLUS 30% to cover possible losses if the stock price goes up, not down.

There are many benefits of Margin for qualifying investors who understand the financial complexities. For example, leverage, immediate line of credit against your portfolio, low interest rates, tax deduction of interest paid.

Example of a Margin Call

Investors with "long" margin positions in falling price markets receive margin calls when the price of their margined securities fall below the minimum maintenance level in their accounts. When that occurs, you get a margin call and have to cover either by selling stock, depositing stock, depositing cash, wiring funds or other cash equivalents. Prompt payment is required. Similar to settlement on purchases in your account.

If you don't settle promptly the broker can sell your positions out to cover the calls.

There are multiple ways margin customers can receive calls. Minimum Maintenance, Minimum Equity, Day Trade, and Fed Regulation T calls. Margin maintenance is typically 30%

Example of a Margin Call

Continuing our $10,000 securities trade example, with a current value of $10,000 with $5,000 of equity and $5,000 of borrowed funds. If the market drops to $8,000 the account now has $3,000 of equity and that's at the border of minimum maintenance of 30% or $3,000.

If the market falls to $7,000 for the securities in our trade example, the account still owes the $5,000 borrowed and only has $2,000 in equity. That's below the 30% or $2,100 ($7,000 x .3) needed to maintain the account and it will receive a margin maintenance call for $100.

If securities prices continue to fall, the account continues to receive margin maintenance calls. If the cash isn't promptly deposited, securities will be automatically sold in the account to cover.

Collapsing markets feed upon themselves.

In collapsing securities markets this causes a downward spiral domino effect.

The banks are selling cash equivalent assets from their securities portfolios to maintain Cap Ratios. This includes the marginable securities (listed above) that the bank owns, causing downward pressure on prices. Meeting the Cap Ration requirements is a dire must of an immediate nature that requires selling off whatever is necessary to avoid being shut down or closed entirely. As the continuing markets plummet the scenario repeats itself over and over in a ripple effect.

The downward market trends on securities prices causes bank Margin customers to require immediate cash payments to cover, often resulting in margin call sell offs which kept leading to more margin calls and more sell offs.

Institutional dumping of stocks, bonds MBS Securities causes the bottom to fall out.

The effect was a veritable collapse and overnight crash of the marketplace for mortgage backed securities, collateralized debt swaps and derivatives.

In this waterfall of downward selling pressure, values plummet. *Fear* of lower prices dried up buyer *interest*. This causes a further resistance to buy and the free fall continue.

The Up-Tick Rule provides support in falling markets

Up until a short time before the Mark to Market was initiated, rules existed to prevent gushing waterfalls of selling pressure from collapsing financial markets. The Securities and Exchange Commission called the policy to support prices and counteract free fall, "the up-tick rule".

The "up-tick rule" was initially instituted by the SEC in 1938[2]. The method in which the up-tick rule prevented free fall was simple, it required a stock's share price on the exchange go up at least 1/8 from the previous trade before one could execute a short sale and sell stock they didn't own; to earn profits on falling prices. The up-tick rule created "support" against spiraling downward price momentum.

Policy change 2:
The second change was the SEC cancelling "the Up-tick Rule". The SEC repealed this rule in a prelude to instituting the Mark to Market. The combination of the two changes was the nearly overnight realization of massive financial disaster.

The "up-tick rule" deserves simple explanation.
The SEC eliminated this rule on July 6, 2007. Whether by coincidence or device, just four short months before the SEC trigger date to mark

---

[2] Confirmed: Securities Exchange Act of 1934 as Rule 10a-1

all the MBS Securitization credit default swap (CDS) and MBS insurance derivatives to market (Mark to Market) that followed in November 2007.

Eliminating the Up-tick Rule meant no supports to the free fall.

As a result, hundreds of commercial, mortgage and investment banks could not meet their Capital Requirements and either were shut down or went bankrupt. Lenders and related corporations who relied on private label securitizing to survive, died an immediate death. Investors including institutions, pension funds, governments, corporations and insurance companies who saw their stock prices plummet to pennies on the dollar caused massive unemployment. Many of the corporations failed. Most if not all of the mortgage brokers and mortgage bankers who originated these toxic investments were obliterated. Massive consolidation of the remaining assets occurred. Previously valuable companies were scooped up by lesser valued companies who artfully retained cash and buying power. The complexion of ownership in the world changed, nearly overnight. Foreclosure is an aspect that individuals continue to fight.

Nitty Gritty of MBS © 2016 Richard M. Kahn

Chapter 6

The Genre and Species of Post 2000 Securitization

Just as a fisherman intent on catching a species must understand them to go after them, it's important to know what type or species of Securitization you are up against in contested litigated foreclosure defense. Once you know the species you are dealing with and want to catch, it becomes critical to know their feeding habits if you want to catch them.

To break down the individual MBS Securitization groups , the simplest way to do it is taxonomic form of Genus, Species and Form. Sounds complicated but as you'll see, it is simple and straightforward.

Nitty Gritty of MBS © 2016 Richard M. Kahn

Post 20000 era Mortgage Backed Securitization (MBS) can be grouped into three basic species.

GENUS: Mortgage Backed Securitization (MBS) can come in two different forms. In our fishing analogy think of it as a fresh water species such as lake trout and a salt water species such as sea trout.

The two forms of MBS are Residential (RMBS) and Commercial (CMBS). The basic difference is the types of real estate properties they include. RMBS includes 1-4 family residences. CMBS includes 5 plus multi-family and commercial properties.

Both RMBS and CMBS are made up of pools of mortgages, financially engineered into securities by mortgage bankers and then sold to investors via Wall Street investment banks. This financial engineering has been referred to previously in the analogy "cows in hamburger out" and specifically as "mortgages in certificates out".

Investors buy the "certificates out" in varying denominations according to their needs.

"Certificates out" are grouped into categories. We call these groups "tranches" in the industry. Tranche is a noun meaning a portion or a slice of something. The tranche groups are related but have different characteristics. For example, different loan maturities or different fixed rate terms, such as 2 year fixed then adjustable, or 5 year fixed then adjustable, or 30 year fixed.

The tranche groups can have different risks. For example, lower or higher credit scores of individual loan borrower mortgages. Or the tranche group can have its risks of default enhanced by pledging other assets or having insurances (detailed in the Credit Enhancement Chapter 17).

The certificates do not represent specific loans.

1. **Species: Private Label Securitization**. Mortgage banks originating and gathering loans in pools, whereupon Wall Street Investment banks sell the financially engineered securities representing ownership interest in the underlying mortgages directly to investors.

   Private label securitized loans undergo credit enhancement and rating by an accredited ratings agency such as Standard & Poor's, Moody's or Fitch. Agency securitizations receive enhancement by the GSEs themselves.

Originating lenders often retain interests in securitized loans via certificate ownership of various levels of the certificates, including the highest risk mortgages on which credit enhancement is not obtained.

The sale to investors and the transferring of mortgages as well as administration and servicing have strict guidelines to adhere to.

Transactions are represented by Agreements and Schedules such as the Pooling and Servicing Agreements, Prospectuses and ancillary filings.

Form: Regulated Mortgage Banks
This sector includes mortgage banks that are regulated by State or Federal regulators and also those that are unregulated.

Form: Unregulated mortgage banks ("a/k/a Lenders")
This sector originates loans, buys loans and sells loans. The difference is that unregulated mortgage banks are not involved with federal or state regulated banking

operations. They do not have depositors or retail bank locations that cater to depositors.

THE BAD APPLE: Unregulated mortgage banks are at the root of the massive defaults that instigated the financial crisis we suffered beginning with the Mortgage Meltdown of 2008, collapse of financial markets, the deep recession and the current foreclosure debacle we continue to experience in the United States. Unregulated mortgage banks are known for sponsoring the subprime loans and alternative documentation loans that.

Unregulated mortgage banks remain at the key component of wrongful foreclosure.

There are 2 Genres in Private Label Securitization: This may be a little tricky in the beginning. There are two genres, one of which enjoys a similar name to the genus. Both are genres for the genus Private Label MBS. One is Publically Traded Private Label MBS and the other is Privately Traded Private Label MBS.

Genre: Publically traded offerings: Required to file and make document and reporting disclosures public in keeping with Security and Exchange Commission rules to protect the public. Any investor with the money and inclination can purchase certificates in Public Offerings.

Genre: Privately traded offerings: Contain strict limitations on the type and financial substance of individual Investors who can buy and sell ownership. Typically limited to investors of an institutional nature. Investors purchasing certificates have to qualify. There are restrictions on purchase and sale. Full disclosures are not required to be made public in with the Securities and Exchange Commission but full reporting is still required to be made to the investors.

2. **Species: GSE Agency Securitization:** The Government Sponsored Enterprise (GSE) securitizations of Fannie Mae[3] and Freddie Mac[4] and other agencies are non-government guaranteed enterprises. Their loan underwriting standards included what is best known as "conforming loans", those

---

[3] Federal National Mortgage Association a/k/a FNMA
[4] Federal Home Loan Mortgage Corporation a/k/a FHLMC

Nitty Gritty of MBS © 2016 Richard M. Kahn

conforming to conventional loan underwriting standards implemented by the GSEs.

Agency organizations are federally chartered but privately owned and operated as corporations. They receive direct and indirect benefits from the U.S. Government in the form of funds and credit that can improve their odds of operating in the marketplace.

The first GSE that was established by the Federal Farm Loan Act of 1916 ("FFLA") enabled a network of farm cooperative lending institutions making direct loans to agriculture related business and residences. In this genre and established in 1988 is the Federal Agricultural Mortgage Corporation ("FAMC" or " Farmer Mac "). While the FFLA lends directly to agricultural, farm related and rural residents; the better known Farmer Mac as acts in a manner similar to Fannie Mae and Freddie Mac in making a secondary marketplace for agricultural and rural housing mortgage loans.

Agency also includes the GSE Government National Mortgage Association ("GNMA" or "Ginnie Mac"). GNMA is one of the GSEs but stands separate and distinct because all the

Nitty Gritty of MBS © 2016 Richard M. Kahn

mortgages contained are either insured or guaranteed with the full faith and credit of the U.S. Government.

3. **Species: Special Purpose Entity ("SPE") Sales.** Also called Bankruptcy Remote or Bank to Bank.:

   Banks and other financial institutions sell mortgages to other banks and financial institutions or aggregators gathering loans up for sale into securitization. This may include other banks or special bankrutcy remote enterprises called Special Purpose Entities (SPEs) or sometimes Qualified Special Purpose Entities (QSPEs).

   The sale of mortgages to other banks and parties interested in securitizing them provides profits and benefits to the seller.

   a. It removes the liability of a mortgage loan from the balance sheet and improves the earnings picture. This benefits the bank's capital ratios and they can borrow more money to make more loans.

   b. It produces up front profit from the sale. Buyers pay a negotiated premium.

c. The bank can retain mortgage servicing rights (MSRs) which represent an annual fee for day to day operations. MSRs can sold for cash or subcontracted out to others for a lower fee than that collected; providing substantial profits in the process.

d. Interest "strips" can produce ongoing revenue in the form of an interest payment differential between the higher payment of the mortgage and the lower payment an investor is willing to accept.

Species MBS Reporting:

A public corporation's annual report filings will detail all their securitization activities, including SPE and QSPE. But the SPE and QSPE are known as "off balance sheet" transactions and as such are not broken down and specifically described. These books and records may only be open to insiders, Accounting firms or Regulators given access.

In securitizations to the public, the SEC is empowered to protect consumers and requires disclosures and documentation to be filed for public access. The SEC requires public corporations file quarterly and annual report filings. These are considered sworn oath federal filings when they are filed. The SEC maintains a public internet access website known as EDGAR as an online search facility for this purpose.

Cross-Species Attribute: Bankruptcy remoteness of mortgage loan sales:

Differences in the process of securitization and the "true sales" involved are at the heart of securitization. True sales are considered "all rights, title and interest".

True sales insure "bankruptcy remote" insulation for the buyer of the mortgage loans (the investor) so that just in case the party who sold the loans goes bankrupt for any reason, the loan(s) that were sold will belong to the buyer. No thread of ownership remains with the seller in a "true sale". All beneficial ownership is sold. The "true sales" are at the heart of securitization to ensure that the investors have the unequivocal legal right of ownership without doubt, to the mortgage assets and receivables in the trust.

It is important to understand each type of securitization when litigating foreclosure. Let's examine them independently.

Nitty Gritty of MBS © 2016 Richard M. Kahn

Chapter 7

Private Label MBS Securitization

In this chapter we are addressing the two types of Private Label Securitization. Those which are publically traded and those which are privately traded.

Mortgage Backed Securities (RMBS) Securitization

The process of collecting a large number of residential real estate secured loans represented by Notes and Mortgages or Deeds of Trusts. Financial engineering then transforms this collection, known as a mortgage pool, by "slicing" up mortgages, either whole or in part and selling certificate interests to investors as securities.

Publically Traded Private Label Securitization Vs. Privately Traded

Publically Traded Private Label Securitization Trusts

If a Private Label MBS Securitization Trust allows sales of certificates to the public and does not restrict transfer, it is a publically traded Private Label Securitization Trust offering and requires registration under the Securities Act of 1933 and any applicable state laws. These MBS Securities certificates can be freely traded in the aftermarket.

In a publically traded offering, access is likely to be available without special permissions.

The deal documents can be found on SEC EDGAR online at http://www.sec.gov/edgar.shtml

"All companies, foreign and domestic, are required to file registration statements, periodic reports, and other forms electronically through EDGAR. Anyone can access and download this information for free. Here you'll find links to a complete list of filings available through EDGAR and instructions for searching the EDGAR database". EDGAR's splash page includes tutorial, search, and other links.

Privately Traded Private Label Securitization Trusts

Private Label privately issued trusts restrict ownership and transfer, made upon reliance on exemption from the Securities Act and such State securities laws that apply. These certificates are known as Restricted Securities.

In order to insure compliance with the Securities Act and other applicable laws, buyers of both initial and transferred Certificates in privately traded private label securitization trusts must certify that they are being issued and sold to "Qualified Institutional Buyers" ("QIBs") SEC Rule 144A allows QIBs to trade securities on the open market. QIBs are considered sophisticated in the eyes of US Securities Regulators.

Qualified Institutional Buyers (QIBs) is are defined in Rule 144A as amended. Buyers must have owned or invested large amounts on a discretionary basis in securities as of the end of the Buyer's most recent fiscal year. This amount is calculated in accordance with Rule 144A. At last check that amount was *"at least $100 million in securities of issuers that are not affiliated with the entity".*

Nitty Gritty of MBS © 2016 Richard M. Kahn

To give you an idea of who these restricted buyers are, QIBs can include insurance companies, investment companies, state plans or agencies for the benefit of its employees, employee benefit plans, trust funds of plans, business development companies defined under the Investment Advisors Act of 1940, qualified 501 C-3 charitable corporations, savings and loans, banks, investment advisers and other qualified institutional buyers. These are all companies that *invested* in MBS Securitizations.

For the record, Registered Investment Companies may be exempt.

When an MBS Securitization is only sold to and the aftermarket certificates only trade among QIBs, the deal documents and particulars will be created but the need to file them with the SEC under Regulation AB disclosure and consumer protection is not required. These are known as "unregistered" MBS Securitizations.

> ➢ Requests for the documentation may be made to the responsible parties in the transaction; usually a law firm on retainer that handles the Trust's business.

- Access permissions may also be necessary for an investigation to review underlying documentation and loan level activity kept by the Master Servicer, Trustee and/or Securities Administrator.

- If you cannot find a record of the transaction on the SEC EDGAR website designed for that purpose, the likelihood is that the deal is privately traded; if the particular deal exists at all. We oftentimes find wrongful foreclosures cases based on trust names that do not exist, or are incorrect. This is a critical finding.

- Interim Securitizers registered with the SEC must still report their purchases and sales of mortgages to both registered and unregistered MBS Securitizations. So an investigator has an opportunity to fact check by enhancing their investigation into these interim transactional parties.

"Registered" MBS Securitizations are also known as "publically traded" and must file their deal documentation with the SEC. This makes them much easier to acquire as opposed to the "unregistered" "privately traded" MBS Securitizations that often require intervention in Court to force Discovery to acquire documents. Both registered and unregistered Private label securitizations may find deal participants filing Shelf Registration document templates with the SEC.

Private Label Securitization pertains to the group of lenders whose subsequent foreclosures are most defendable in a contested wrongful foreclosure lawsuit. These include both registered and unregistered.

Private Label MBS Securitization of both genres (Publically traded and Privately traded) includes regulated and unregulated mortgage bank loan origination and securitization. Unregulated mortgage lenders were the initial Bad Apple that tainted the entire basket of MBS Securitization of mortgage loans. Unregulated mortgage banks earnings quickly caused other securitizers to lower their standards and follow in that earning path. Regulated and unregulated lenders were and remain at the core of wrongful foreclosure activities by successor loan servicers.

Other than this caveat of available documentation to combat a litigated foreclosure, both Privately Traded and Publically Traded Private Label Securitizations are formed in the same way. So we can group their manner of formation together.

In Private Label Securitization there are several parties and several "true sales" that the initial original loan documents will pass through on their way to the final vault location with the Document Custodian.

Note and Mortgage: Borrower to Originator, then true sale to Sponsor; Then true sale to Depositor; Then SPV mortgages in, Certificates as securities out with loan documents to the Document Custodian and; then true sale to the MBS Trust of investors.

In the Private Label Securitization model the Note and Mortgage/ Deed of Trust are originated then sold to multiple parties along the chain of ownership to the final MBS Securitization Trust of investors.

Let's summarize the sale typical loan origination process .

1. **Origination.** Borrower takes a loan out, signs a Note and gives a Mortgage or Deed of Trust as security for repayment of the Note.
   - A Deed of Trust is the name of a Mortgage in a State whose foreclosure process does not require appearance in Court, known as the judicial process.
   - In judicial process the security instrument is a Mortgage.
   - In non-judicial process the borrower agrees that the lender does not have to sue in court for foreclosure, the lender

can merely post notice and foreclose without going to court.

- Different States have different processes. Many non-judicial states can move to a judicial process if the borrower shows cause in Court. Borrower's side legal counsel in a state know the legal rules.

2. **True Sale 1:** Originating Lender sells mortgage loans individually or in groups to a Sponsor who is collecting a/k/a "aggregating" loans in pools that they will sell;

3. **True Sale 2:** Sponsor sells mortgage loans individually or in groups to the securitizing Depositor, who:
   - creates bankruptcy remote Special Purpose Entity (SPE);
   - takes loans in;
   - enhances the borrower's credit to investment grade;
   - slices up the pool of mortgages into different groups;
   - financially engineers the different groups of mortgages into securities represented by "book entry" ownership certificates that are not linked to specific loans in the pool.
   - delivers the properly endorsed Notes and assigned Mortgages (the holder in due course originals) to the Document

Nitty Gritty of MBS © 2016 Richard M. Kahn

Custodian. The Document Custodian puts the file boxes of valuable originals into its vaults;

- Requests for holder in due course original Notes and Mortgages in litigated foreclosure cases should go to the Document Custodian. The Document Custodian may be a separate entity or a Master Loan Servicer. More detail on this in a subsequent chapter.

4. **True Sale 3:** Depositor sells the entire group of mortgage loans to the Trust of Investors that they will purchase. The Trust of investors is represented by a Trustee.

ORIGINATION

In the private label securitization the lender decides the underwriting parameters of the mortgages. "Winning Against Foreclosure – A Strategy Guide" covered the scheme of designing predatory loan programs that appeared to be excellent long term solutions but in fact were predictably toxic. In brief, these included

- Payment Option Adjustable Rate Mortgages,
- Negative Amortization (the principal increases to a maximum percentage – such as 110-125% of initial loan amount),
- Recasting – when a low interest loan hits a certain trigger such as time or increased loan amount it converts to a high interest

loan that is difficult or impossible to refinance when equity does not exist in the property. This usually occurs at either 5 years or the maximum principal accumulation occurs. Then the terms are changed automatically to a fixed or adjustable rate loan on the balance of years amortization due with full interest and principal paid each month.

- No Income, No Asset;
- Stated Income, Stated Asset;
- No Income, No Asset.

LOAN SERVICING

Private Label securitizations allow retaining loan servicing and using outsource providers to coordinate all aspects of the transactions from origination through default loan servicing and foreclosure. Subsidiaries or related companies perform loan servicing. In the final exit strategy of foreclosure, lenders manipulate borrowers and investors who purchased the loans and steer foreclosure to related parties for even more profit.

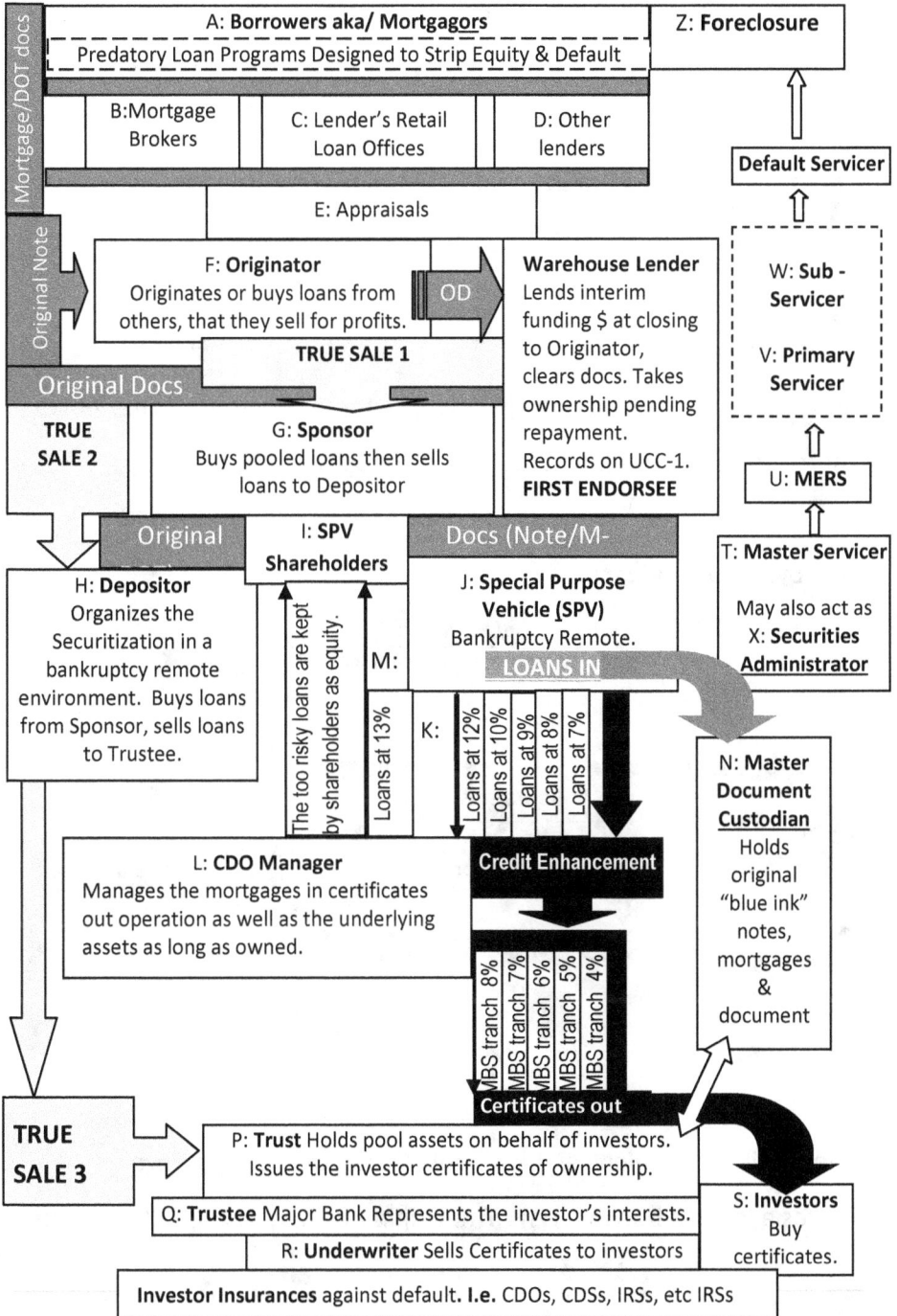

A: Borrowers aka/ Mortgagors			Z: Foreclosure

Predatory Loan Programs Designed to Strip Equity & Default

Mortgage/DOT docs

B: Mortgage Brokers	C: Lender's Retail Loan Offices	D: Other lenders

Default Servicer

E: Appraisals

Original Note

F: Originator
Originates or buys loans from others, that they sell for profits.

OD

TRUE SALE 1

Warehouse Lender
Lends interim funding $ at closing to Originator, clears docs. Takes ownership pending repayment. Records on UCC-1.
FIRST ENDORSEE

W: **Sub - Servicer**

V: **Primary Servicer**

Original Docs

TRUE SALE 2

G: Sponsor
Buys pooled loans then sells loans to Depositor

U: **MERS**

Original   I: **SPV Shareholders**   **Docs (Note/M-**

T: **Master Servicer**

H: Depositor
Organizes the Securitization in a bankruptcy remote environment. Buys loans from Sponsor, sells loans to Trustee.

J: Special Purpose Vehicle (SPV)
Bankruptcy Remote.
LOANS IN

May also act as X: **Securities Administrator**

M: The too risky loans are kept by shareholders as equity.

M: Loans at 13%

K: Loans at 12% | Loans at 10% | Loans at 9% | Loans at 8% | Loans at 7%

N: **Master Document Custodian**
Holds original "blue ink" notes, mortgages & document

L: CDO Manager
Manages the mortgages in certificates out operation as well as the underlying assets as long as owned.

Credit Enhancement

MBS tranch 8% | MBS tranch 7% | MBS tranch 6% | MBS tranch 5% | MBS tranch 4%

Certificates out

TRUE SALE 3

P: Trust Holds pool assets on behalf of investors. Issues the investor certificates of ownership.

S: **Investors**
Buy certificates.

Q: **Trustee** Major Bank Represents the investor's interests.

R: **Underwriter** Sells Certificates to investors

Investor Insurances against default. I.e. CDOs, CDSs, IRSs, etc IRSs

Let's look at the private label securitization in visual steps illustrated in the author's diagram at left, then go through each group of steps.

The basis of catching faulty chain of title in a litigated foreclosure action is often discovered when parties seeking to foreclose misrepresent ownership entirely or skip links in the chain.

In the following illustrations , anywhere the boxes touch other boxes there is a relationship. The flow is from top to bottom.

Borrower to Originator:

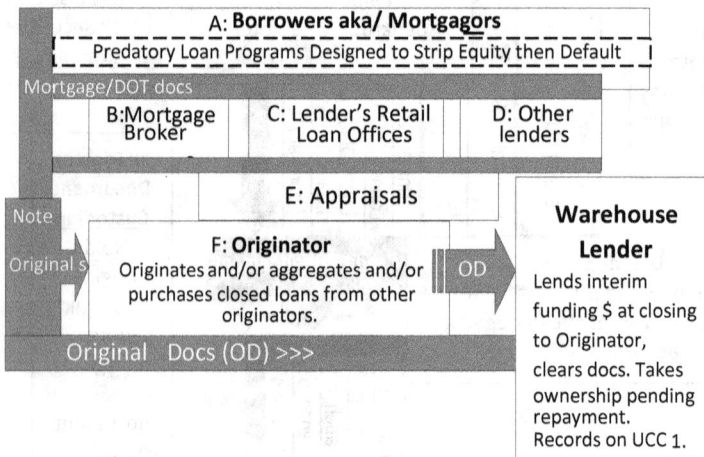

A: Borrowers aka/ Mortgagors		
Predatory Loan Programs Designed to Strip Equity then Default		
B:Mortgage Broker	C: Lender's Retail Loan Offices	D: Other lenders
E: Appraisals		

Mortgage/DOT docs

Note

Original s

F: Originator
Originates and/or aggregates and/or purchases closed loans from other originators.

OD

Warehouse Lender

Lends interim funding $ at closing to Originator, clears docs. Takes ownership pending repayment. Records on UCC 1.

Original   Docs (OD) >>>

The Originator, which can be a bank, lender or mortgage broker, makes a loan to borrower(s). The Originator may also purchase loans originated to borrowers by others. In these ways the Originator obtains a loan including the borrower(s) signed original documents. Note, Mortgage or Deed of Trust, Other legal documents and disclosures.

Sale 1 occurs when using a warehouse lender

A Warehouse Lender is typically involved as an interim party, lending money to the Originator. Warehouse lenders receive an endorsed Note and typically record interim ownership on UCC-1. This is not a true sale, meaning bankruptcy remote from the Originator. (Detailed in the Warehouse Lending chapter 9).

True Sale 1: Originator to Sponsor

The Originator sells individual or multiple loans to the Sponsor, who accumulates the loans into large pools of loans for sale to the Depositor. Aggregate pool loan amounts can range to hundreds of millions and often over $1 billion dollars per MBS Securitization.

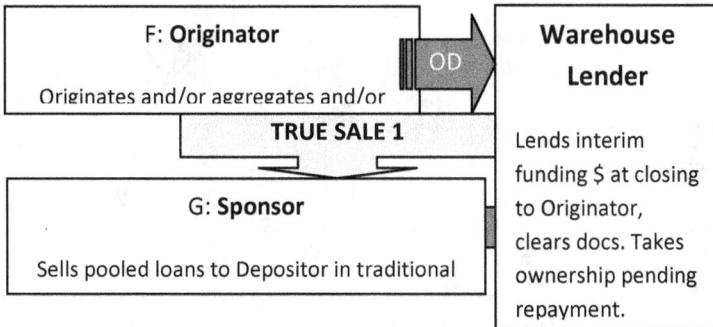

F: Originator	Warehouse Lender
Originates and/or aggregates and/or	Lends interim funding $ at closing to Originator, clears docs. Takes ownership pending repayment.
TRUE SALE 1	
G: Sponsor	
Sells pooled loans to Depositor in traditional	

Nitty Gritty of MBS © 2016 Richard M. Kahn

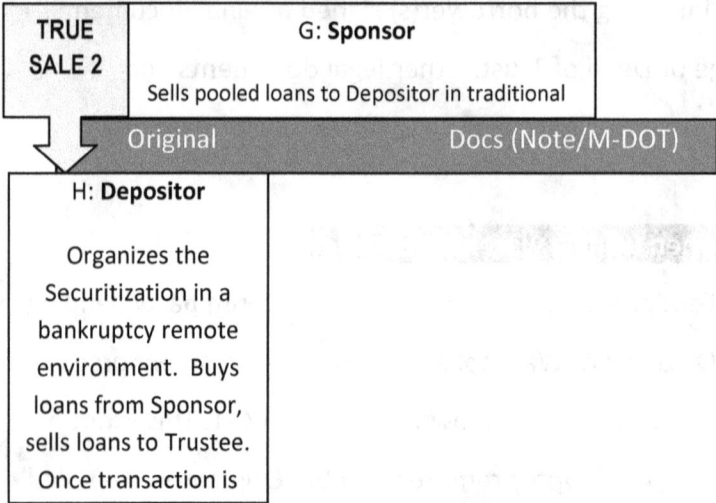

TRUE SALE 2	G: **Sponsor**
	Sells pooled loans to Depositor in traditional
Original	Docs (Note/M-DOT)

H: **Depositor**

Organizes the Securitization in a bankruptcy remote environment. Buys loans from Sponsor, sells loans to Trustee. Once transaction is

The Financial Engineering of Mortgages In Certificates (Securities)

Out, occurs in between True Sale 2 and True Sale 3.

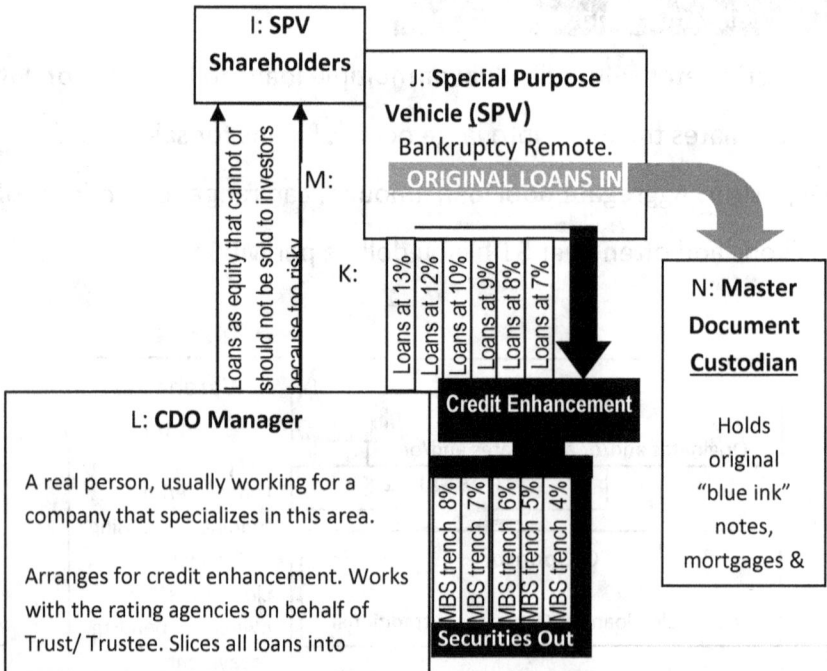

I: **SPV Shareholders**

J: **Special Purpose Vehicle (SPV)**
Bankruptcy Remote.
ORIGINAL LOANS IN

M:

Loans as equity that cannot or should not be sold to investors because too risky

K:

Loans at 13%
Loans at 12%
Loans at 10%
Loans at 9%
Loans at 8%
Loans at 7%

Credit Enhancement

N: **Master Document Custodian**

Holds original "blue ink" notes, mortgages &

L: **CDO Manager**

A real person, usually working for a company that specializes in this area.

Arranges for credit enhancement. Works with the rating agencies on behalf of Trust/ Trustee. Slices all loans into

MBS trench 8%
MBS trench 7%
MBS trench 6%
MBS trench 5%
MBS trench 4%

Securities Out

The SPV offers Shareholder ownership to participants. The Sponsor providing the aggregated mortgages and the Depositor organizing the securitization each own shares in the SPV. Fees and profits received in the SPV loans in, securities out process are split up as agreed in writing under the shareholder's agreement.

This process includes the bankruptcy remote Special Purpose Entity (SPE), in this case called a Special Purpose Vehicle (SPV) that is created for the purpose of facilitating the "financial engineering" of "mortgages in – securities out".

SPV, Special Purpose Vehicle

The Depositor creates or uses an existing "shell" (no real operations or assets) company called the Special Purpose Vehicle (SPV). The SPV exists only briefly. The Depositor sells all the loans in the pool that it acquired from the Sponsor, to the SPV in true sales, meaning properly endorsed Notes and recorded Assignments of Mortgage/DOT.

In Private Label securitizations the originating and aggregating lender has their hands in every phase of the SPE model. To differentiate the Private Label SPE we are discussing in this chapter from the SPE bank to bank model to be discussed in an upcoming chapter, we will refer to the SPE it by its synonymous name: SPV, Special Purpose Vehicle.

It should be noted while Private Label securitizations utilize SPVs, Agency GSE securitizations (Fannie Mae, Freddie Mac, etc) covered in their upcoming chapters do not utilize the SPE/SPV bankruptcy remote enterprise in their GSE MBS securitization process.

You will recognize the term SPE as one of the three Species of MBS Securitizations referenced in the prior Chapter (7). SPE is also referred to as QSPE or SPV or bank to bank. The names are synonymous. The different arbitrary use of names shouldn't confuse you. The SPE performs the same functions and operate in the same fashion

> When the sales occur in a process that the bank is not involved with the securitization, the SPE sales are a separate accounting category.

- Banks often purchase certificates in the event the loans become securitized in the process.

Aggregators: In Species 3: MBS Securitization called QSPE or Bank to Bank off balance sheet sales, the party(s) to whom the sales are made often step in here, and pick up performing the MBS securitization in the same way. In this case the Aggregator is called a Securitizer and is required to file loan acquisition and sales reporting with the SEC. This is often a source of information in litigated foreclosures.

In the Private Label securitizations the SPE is controlled by the related parties. When we get to the SPE or bank to bank securitizations chapter we'll find that regulatory rules and accounting standards require the originating lender stay out of the securitization enterprise.

The SPE/SPV is key to the "bankruptcy remote" enterprise.
It is created to shield the mortgage assets from bankruptcy of the sellers and potential claims by creditors of the sellers. This is a typical criteria of the investors who want to know that the loans they buy are theirs. Investors do not want risk of ownership linked back to the sellers to potentially lose the properties should the sellers go bankrupt. In a seller bankruptcy without that true sale protection the investors can watch the underlying security interests revert back to the sellers.

Two functions the SPV performs are:
1. Upgrades borrower credit to investment grade with the help of the CDO Manager;

2. Convert the "mortgage" loan asset into a security "Certificate" asset that can be sold over and over again purporting to represent particular identified mortgage assets when that is hardly the case.

The SPV is established to own and hold the entire collateral of pooled loans and issue the securities in the form of certificates for only an instant in time. The SPV is a transaction enterprise for the purpose at a closing table to facilitate the securitization. The SPV typically includes no business location, has actual employees and no life before or after the "mortgages in – securities certificates out" transaction.

For those few moments in time the SPV is in existence to facilitate a transaction at a closing table, the SPV has tremendous assets. So it's hard to catch it with any tangible worth unless you're at that closing table or get to them at that time. By definition, that's not possible in the foreclosure situation because once the Private Label securitization trust takes ownership at the closing table the SPV has no assets remaining.

Although the SPV has no assets coming in or going out, for the brief hours of a closing, it is the recorded owner of the entire pool of mortgages representing hundreds of millions and very often over one billion in mortgage assets in each individual MBS Securitized Trust. The exact amounts depend on the size of the loan pools being purchased by investors.

The key in the SPV transaction is True Sales

True sales are the heart and soul of bankruptcy remoteness. When one buys an intangible asset like a mortgage loan, they want to ensure that they own each loan in full, without possible claims from creditor's of sellers who my become bankrupt. The owners pay full face value of the mortgage plus a premium, all in cash for each mortgage asset they purchase.

Bankruptcy remote true sale means no claims can be made by the seller to the asset after it is sold. No claims by creditors of that seller can be made against the sold asset. True sale represents "all rights, title and interest", properly negotiated, assigned, delivered, accepted and acknowledged. This enable the asset to be truly "bankruptcy remote".

There is one residual evidence of the SPV transaction, the endorsement on the Note from the selling Sponsor to the purchasing Depositor and the endorsement from the Depositor to the Private

Label securitization MBS Trust. Most Private Label securitization agreements require these "intervening endorsements."

➤ This is an important evidentiary issue in litigated foreclosure cases.

The Depositor then engages a CDO Manager who performs the financial engineering of mortgage loans in, tradable securities in the form or Certificates out.

The CDO Manager is a "Life of Loans" manager to the trust of investors. The CDO Manager is a real person, usually working for their own company or a company that specializes in CDO Management.

The SPV purchases all loans in true sales of all rights, title and interest. The Collateralized Debt Obligations ("CDO") Manger facilitates proper individual mortgage loan documentation is provided, including endorsements, recordation of true sales and assignments of Mortgages. The CDO Manager may rely on a Warehouse Lender's representation that loans sold are "dry" and ready to go. (Detailed in Warehouse Lending, Chapter 9).

Mortgages In Certificates Out. Once the original mortgage loan documents are delivered to the Document Custodian, the CDO Manager creates the certificates representing tranches or shares.

Interest Stripping

The CDO Manager calculates the higher borrower interest being paid on loans against the lower interest rate requirements of investors. Then, taking into consideration any interest or principal required for the Credit Enhancement needs, the CDO Manager strips off any excess interest and principal not required for the deal at hand, placing it to the side. This excess interest and/or principal will be packaged and sold separately for additional profits to the Securitizers. (Detailed in the Interest Strips, Chapter 18).

Derivative Securitization

The process of securitizing loans in this manner may be referred to as Derivative Securitization. For example, Collateralized Debt Obligations (CDOs) created by the RMBS Securitization process

The CDO Manager slices all loans into different groups called "tranches", each representing different grades of certificates. For example, Super Senior, Senior, Mezzanine, Subordinated a/k/a Equity. These offer different credit risks and returns. "A" to "AAA" for Senior tranches down to "B" to "BBB" for Mezzanine and different maturities. Below those ratings or equivalents depending on the terminology of an individual Ratings Agency, the certificates are not considered investment grade.

The CDO Manager facilitates credit enhancement and/or subordination to raise the credit ratings of the certificates being offered. Enhancing the credit of the underlying borrowers often includes pledging or attaching different derivative investments, excess interest from mortgage loans, credit default swaps or insurances against default of mortgage loans in the pool or, as additional security. (Detailed in Credit Enhancement, Chapter 17).

The CDO Manager works with the rating agencies such as Moody's, S&P, and Fitch, on behalf of the Private Label securitization MBS Trust's Trustee. The purpose of this process is to raise the credit of individual borrower's loans within the groups so that Certificates offered will enjoy investment quality debt ratings such as Moody's, S&P or Fitch "A to AAA" or the equivalent.

True Sale 2 is Paid Off is in Cash *and* Equity.
The cash is paid by investors. The sale in the form of a "simultaneous transaction" between the Investors payment of cash and the payment to the Depositor. On top of the cash, equity ownership comes in the form of investor securities (Certificates) on sliced up loans whose borrower credit was simply too poor to be credit enhanced up to Investment Grade. Equity can come in other forms such as interest

strips or par plus sales and higher rated securities. The Depositor will benefit financially from sales to others of these stripped off assets.

Interest Strip Profits: Retention of spreads between the higher borrower mortgage payment and lower interest yield required by the Investor on investment grade securities. Example: Loan rate 8%, Yield to Investors 6%; Ongoing profit 2%. (Detailed in Interest Strips, Chapter 18).

Principal resale profits: When loans are sold as securities paying lower yields to investors than the higher interest paid on the loan by borrowers, principal profits from the sale occurs. Example: Investors paying $50,000 to receive the interest rate stripped out.

After Consummation of the Loans In, Securities Out, the SPV has zero assets. After the SPV issues the credit enhanced securities, these are then sold to a group of individual Investors formed in a MBS Securitized Trust. The Trust is represented by a Trustee who conducts the MBS Securitized Trust business on behalf of the investor owners. The SPV's purpose of existence is now complete.

Three Phases of CDO Management

The CDO Manager manages the loan assets through their life or until the pool closes, whichever happens first. These assets are known as either "Static" or "Managed". In Static, the collateral is fixed through the life of the CDO. In Managed, there is a Portfolio Manager (PM) appointed to actively manage the CDO's collateral. There are three phases of this operation.

The Initial Phase: Ramping up. May last about a year. The PM invests initial proceeds from sales of certificates representing the security interest that investors bought. These may be invested in other CDOs and/or pass through certificates.

The Middle Phase: Active Management. PM reinvests cash flows, buys and sells assets and actively manages the CDOs collateral.

The End Phase: Winding Down. As the collateral matures or is otherwise taken off the books (foreclosure for example), the investors are paid until there is no more collateral or the investors are paid off completely.

The CDO Manager in a managed transaction is reinvesting cash flow, selling and buying assets. Investors often do not know which specific loans the CDO manager will invest in. While the pool of mortgages themselves is designed to be static, meaning restricting purchases of sales of additional mortgage loans after the cutoff date.

The CDO Manager is identified in deal documents, so investors know the identity of that company or individual. The filings may include the investment guidelines the CDO Manager will operate under. Investors run the risk of poor CDO Management and credit risk on the assets. The wholesale enhancement of what has turned out to be poor borrower credit, akin to Junk Bond ratings yet upgraded to AAA investment grade, provides additional reasons not to modify a loan.

The CDO Manager gives the original mortgage loan documents to the Document Custodian. The Depositor endorses the Notes and assigns the Mortgages it purchased. The CDO Manager causes the SPV to deliver the pool of original loan documents to a Document Custodian for safe keeping.

Private Label Securitization Document Custody can be horrific. Document Custodians in Private Label Securitizations are under far less rigid guidelines than those approved by Agency GSEs (Fannie Mae, Freddie Mac and Ginnie Mae).

Unlike GSE Document Custody Protocols with vaults, high level access security and established Protocols, Private Label Document Custodians often throw document files into boxes and line those up wherever convenient. This shoddy process is a root cause of original loan documents being destroyed, lost or stolen.

Holding hundreds of Billions of dollars of Notes endorsed in blank. In addition to Notes endorsed to specific parties, the Document Custodian stores "bearer" instruments in the form of Notes endorsed "pay to the order of _____"; and signed by the seller. These are negotiable by anyone who has them in their possession.

➢ In a contested foreclosure the absence of original loan documents combined with a lack of evidence in proving chain of title without doubt, Investors are at risk of not being able to enforce or bring foreclosure.

➢ Holder in due course properly perfected original Notes and mortgages should be requested from the Document Custodian.

Nitty Gritty of MBS © 2016 Richard M. Kahn

The CDO Manager is a direct pipeline to savvy investors.
Lenders and financial institutions can swoop in and buy up negotiated mortgage assets which have defaulted; paying pennies on the dollar and then foreclose and sell the property for profits. Or, they can negotiate the loan terms that work for a borrower and create a seasoned payment history; then resell the loan as a performing loan for profits. We refer to this latter process as Loan Extraction.

CDO Managers are often affiliated with the Originating Lender and/or Sponsor. A CDO Manager's motivation may not be revealed.

CDO Managers are prime sources for "scratch and dent" mortgage loan insider deals. Buying and selling defaulted mortgage loans for pennies on the dollar is a valuable commodity.

Scratch and dent mortgage loans are those in default where there may be substantial opportunity to capture large capital gains by either foreclosing at prices below market price, renegotiating financing that becomes performing with the borrower or selling the loan to an aggressive default servicing company who does this for a living.

Substantial profit opportunities exist to these regulated institutions in the "scratch and dent" loan marketplace. Default loan servicing and foreclosure phase servicers are often the same ones whose counterparties originally hired the CDO Manager.

When the CDO Manager says "I've got buyers for these defaulted loans, give me some product", the Default loan servicing and foreclosure phase servicers see dollar signs and crack the whip on their foreclosure enterprises. This stimulates the "foreclosure by any means" mentality, even if it includes falsifying documents and lying in court to do so.

Arbitrage deals

Defaulted "scratch and dent" loans can offer a very attractive opportunity for money managers but the credit does not meet investment grade debt.

Institutions that are limited in the type of debt they can buy have other ways of getting in on picking up scratch and dent deals on loans where the credit ratings do not even meet those of the lowest rated junk bond debt. Minimum debt grade "investment quality or better" may provide purchase limitations from regulatory agencies or corporate policy restrictions. It is not just a bank that may be under

Nitty Gritty of MBS © 2016 Richard M. Kahn

these restrictions; pension funds, insurance companies, mutual funds also find themselves restricted in "how low can they go".

Defaulted loans can trade in the Over the Counter (OTC) commodities markets

All one needs in the unregulated Over the Counter (OTC) derivatives marketplace is a willing buyer and seller. Remember, mortgages, even defaulted ones, are big ticket items. That means high trading commissions even when the actual percentage fees are fractional. It also means big potential profits. A package of scratch and dent loans may include hundreds, thousands; even millions of dollars of potential profit.

Unfortunately, 'easy money' is in the "foreclose and sell" process.

Seasoning loans on new terms is a timely process with the ups and downs of individual borrower situations to consider. Savvy "scratch and dent" loan buyers with money behind them are smart to foreclose and sell at fire sale prices. From the investor point of view, the object is providing extraordinary profits to shareholders in eighteen to thirty six months. It is not keeping homeowners in their homes.

H: Depositor

Organizes the Securitization in a bankruptcy remote environment. Buys loans from Sponsor, sells loans to Trustee. Once transaction is

N: Master Document Custodian

Holds original "blue ink" notes, mortgages & document

L: CDO Manager
Manages the mortgages in certificates out operation as well as the underlying assets as long as owned.

Credit Enhancement

MBS tranch 8%
MBS tranch 7%
MBS tranch 6%
MBS tranch 5%
MBS tranch 4%

Certificates out

TRUE SALE 3

P: Trust Holds pool assets on behalf of investors. Issues the investor certificates of ownership.

S: Investors Buy certificates.

Q: Trustee Major Bank Represents the investor's interests.

R: Underwriter Sells Certificates to investors

Investor Insurances against default. I.e. CDOs, CDSs, IRSs, etc IRSs

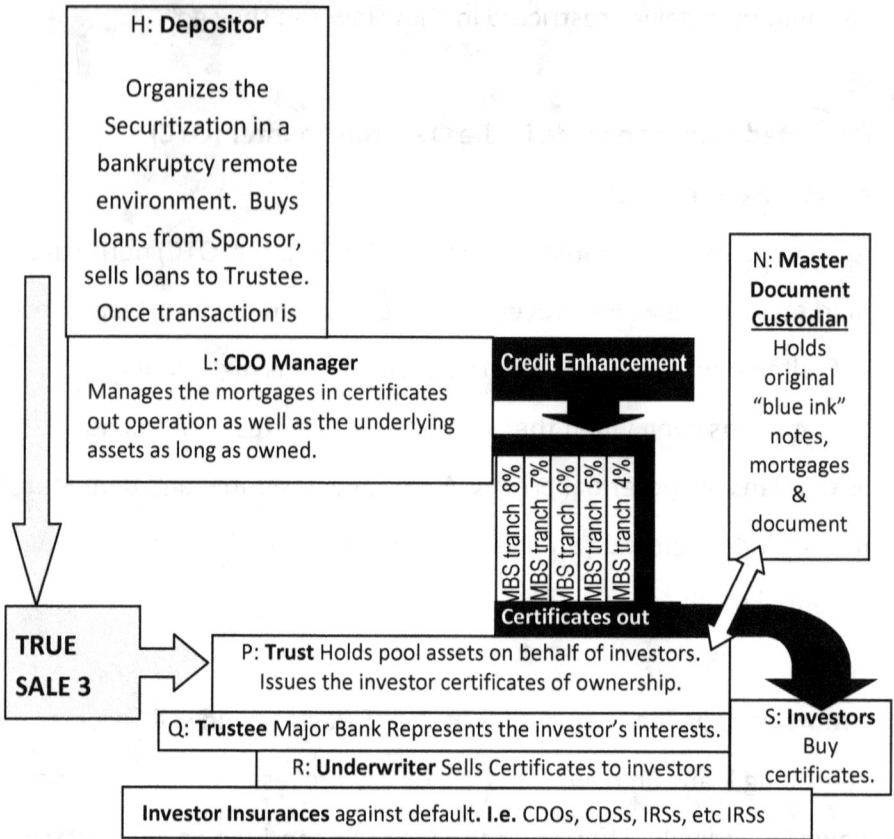

The trust of investors pays cash, or cash equivalent (wired funds for example) when they purchase the certificates of ownership in the MBS Securitization Trust. Each pool is in the hundreds of millions, or billions of dollars. Closing takes place on a specific day, called the Closing Date or Startup Date.

In Private Label Securitization, the legal deal agreements supersede the terms of the underlying loan documents themselves. Publically traded Private Label deal documents are required to be filed with the SEC under their rules of disclosure (Regulation AB). These documents often encompass many hundreds, even thousands of pages. They are written in "legalese", heavily cross referenced in texts, exhibits and addendums, making it extremely difficult for an investor or securities broker to understand.

Servicing & Security Administration manage day to day operations.

Master Loan Servicing
Responsibility for all day to day loan administrative activities between the borrowers and investors are conducted by a Master Loan Servicer formally inaugurated into the securities documentation of the investor Trust.

Sub-Servicing
While the Master Loan Servicer is ultimately accountable, they rarely perform the actual duties of loan servicing to the borrower. That job is delegated to sub-servicers or specialized default loan servicers which may encompass several sub-servicing layers.

Evidence of Servicer Authority

Nitty Gritty of MBS © 2016 Richard M. Kahn

Loan servicers evidence authority to service by holding a copy (certified to the original or not) of initial original Note and M/DOT. These are not the current owner's properly endorsed originals with perfected ownership that are in the hands of the Master Document Custodian. Loan servicers are third party vendors.

Loan Servicer Financial Interest is Measurable. Normally servicing fees are in the fraction of one percent of loan amount range. Percentages are spelled out in servicing agreements. In publically traded Private Label MBS these will be in the deal documents required to be filed with the S.E.C. If layers of sub-servicing exists, they often sell and assign their servicing rights to others for fees and profits in the process.

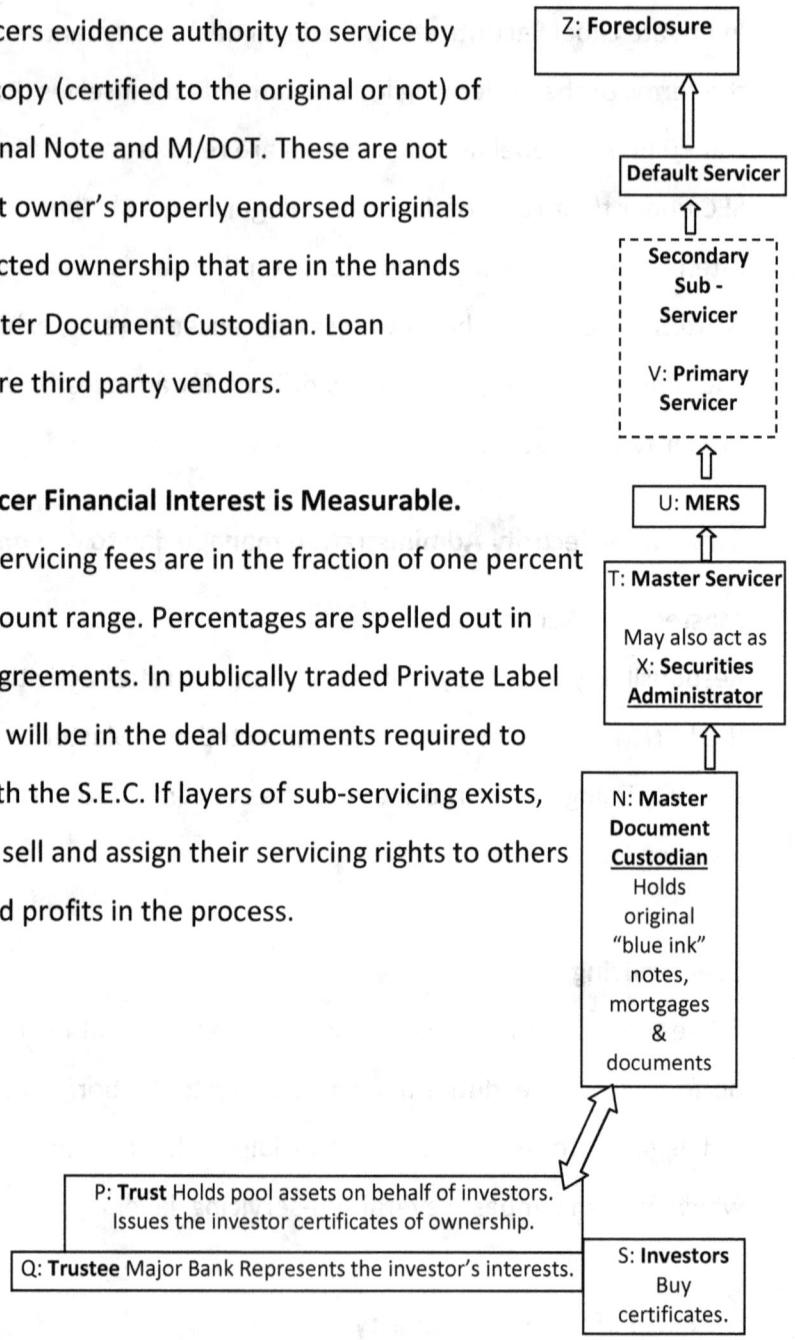

Z: **Foreclosure**

Default Servicer

Secondary Sub - Servicer

V: **Primary Servicer**

U: **MERS**

T: **Master Servicer**

May also act as X: **Securities Administrator**

N: **Master Document Custodian** Holds original "blue ink" notes, mortgages & documents

P: **Trust** Holds pool assets on behalf of investors. Issues the investor certificates of ownership.

Q: **Trustee** Major Bank Represents the investor's interests.

S: **Investors** Buy certificates.

Nitty Gritty of MBS © 2016 Richard M. Kahn

For example, a Master Servicer earns ½ of one percent a year for loan servicing. It sells servicing to a primary sub-servicer who accepts 3/8ths of one percent to do the job. The Master Servicer retains a 1/8 interest. This sub-servicing process may include named positions. For instance, Master Servicer, Primary, Secondary, et cetera.

When a Loan Servicer is actually a Loan's Owner such as an Originator, the Loan Servicing/Owner may also retain a measurable financial interest in the form of an "interest strip". The difference between the spread on a higher borrower interest payment over a lower interest yield requirement payable to investors. For example, an 8% mortgage payment vs. a 7% yield paid to investors.

Generally speaking, Loan Servicers are not Owners in MBS Securitization, even if servicing is retained.

Default Loan Servicing

Loans which are defaulted, considered to be 91 or more days late, are serviced differently than performing loans. They require the servicer in many instances to pay or arrange payment of escrows such as taxes and forced place insurances. They also require such services as ongoing checks on the property, care and maintenance. From a legal perspective they involve insuring the property is actively being or in is in the process of foreclosure.

MERS

MERS is an acronym the Mortgage Electronic Registration System. Depending on the loan servicing contracts, the loan servicer may be the designated party responsible to act as the MERS nominee on the mortgage. Lawful owners of loans often endow servicers in this capacity. In this way the mortgage portion of the loan can be transferred to another servicer without undergoing recordation in the local state property records where the property is located each time the mortgage loan servicing is transferred. Thereby avoiding substantial actual fees and administrative costs attributed to a proper assignment process by staff. The MERS executive keeping the record up to date is an employee of the current sub-servicer. (Detailed in MERS, Chapter 16).

MERS never has any Attributes of Ownership whatsoever.

MERS never acquires the true owner's ownership interest by which MERS now can step forward with the properly perfected true owner's documentary evidence of ownership.

➢ False claims of transfer and MERS created assignment documents are one of the root causes of and findings in wrongful foreclosures.

MERS in Non-Judicial States

In non-judicial process states which allow foreclosure to be conducted without the presentation of the perfected current owner's properly endorsed original note, a Mortgage, called a Deed of Trust (DOT), with MERS as nominee may be all that is needed.

Compliance with written agreements is often disregarded. It is critical in the initial securitization process for the securitizing parties to comply strictly with the written agreements and proper endorsements and assignments of initial original documentation.

➢ In wrongful foreclosure we often find lack of compliance with written MBS Securitization deal documents and a break in the proper chains of title.

Servicers must legally demonstrate their rights and evidentiary basis to substantiate claims they are the holder of the DOT or are the holder's agent. The evidence must demonstrate that the Note and

DOT were transferred to the Trust in order to demonstrate that the party claiming to be the servicer is indeed the servicer of the Note.

The Master Servicer has access to the Document Custodian
Requests are made to the Document Custodian for original properly transferred loan ownership documentation. Essentially this is the properly endorsed Note and assigned Mortgage. In non-judicial states it can also include Substitutions of the initial Trustee on the DOT who is empowered to take actions on behalf of the borrower and Lender under its terms. Original documents are paramount to demonstrate unequivocal ownership under the agreements.
Document Custodian originals are also used by loan Servicers to prove authority that the servicer is indeed the servicer of the Note.

Securities Administrator
This is the entity that handles the day to day securities administration to the investor side of the equation. The Master Loan Servicer often also acts as the Securities Administrator. In this dual role there is a seamless relation of data integrity from the borrower to the investor.

Trustee
A Trustee, usually a large and substantial financial institution is responsible for money and reporting integrity to the investors. The

Trustee is the party responsible to the investors. Communications on investor interests to outside parties occurs through the Trustee.

Outsource Providers

Monolithic outsource providers maintain servicer and securities administrator platforms designed to seamlessly integrate all processes from borrower taking and holding a mortgage loan to investor's owning and collecting revenue from that loan.

This includes master loan and sub servicing, securities administration and trustee activities. It also may include collection of borrower payments on delinquent loans to foreclosure legal actions.

Outsource providers synchronize activity of the entire securitization process from Origination to maintaining Trustee reporting and payment to Investors.

Chapter 8

Private Label Table Funding and Par Plus

Table Funding

The mortgage banker originating the loan in a table funding transaction is not funding the loan at all, they are underwriting the loan to the third party lender's guidelines and the loan is closing in the broker's name but at the closing table the loan is transferred to the lender who simultaneously funds the loan.

In a table funding scenario you will see the name of the broker who was approved as a wholesale lending originator by the funding lender appear on the loan origination documents.

Table funding is different from Warehouse Lending which will be covered in the next chapter. Both table funding and warehouse lending use the terms "dry" and "wet" but in Table Funding the terms have different meanings than those in Warehouse Lending. They table funding meanings of "wet" and "dry" are opposite to their use in warehouse lending.

In this chapter we will concentrate on Table Funding.

In table funding the terms "wet funding" and "dry funding" are used. States determine which process is allowed.

Dry Funding or Dry Settlement
Refers to a loan closing that does not require all the loan documents to be completed. Loan proceeds are not distributed at the time of signing all the closing documents. In Dry Funding the signing of documents occurs on a different day than the actual loan closing. There is a lag of time in order to make sure that all the closing loan documents required for funding are complete.

Dry Funding states employ a kind of laid back or cooling off approach to mortgage funding. Once the funding lender reviews and disperses the funds to the title company, they disperse the funds to the Seller (in a purchase), the new lender (in a refinance) with any additional funds to the borrower (refinance with cash out).

Alphabetically, Alaska, Arizona, California, Hawaii, Idaho, Nevada, New Mexico, Oregon and Washington States permitted Dry Funding. This is opposite to the meaning of "dry" in Warehousing. In warehousing "dry" means all documents in and ready to be sold or transferred to another party purchasing the loan from the Originator or interim owner.

Wet Funding or Wet Settlement

All those States not previously mentioned in the previous dry funding section are "Wet Funding" states.

Wet Funding is a fast closing process. All the underwriting requirements are completed before or at the time of closing. The documents are signed. Funds are transferred to the title company and funding is dispersed. To the Seller in a purchase. In a refinance, funds may be held for dispersing in compliance with the 3 day right of rescission on a refinance if it is applicable. Refinance rights of rescission apply when a new lender is refinancing a loan of a different lender.

Table Funding is a Simultaneous Transaction

Table funding approved originating mortgage Broker has borrower sign the loan documents. Broker sells the loan, endorsing the Note over to the simultaneously purchasing Lender who provides the funds to actually close the loan at the closing table.

Table funding is different than Warehouse Lending
In warehouse lending which we delve into next chapter, the loan originator closes in their own name using borrowed funds from a warehouse line of credit they have. Usually with a commercial bank. Lender can retain loan ownership and service the loan for a time or sell the loan with servicing released.

Par Plus of Yield Spread Premium (YSP)
When the originator is a Broker as in Table Funding, the Broker can increase the fees they earn on a loan origination by up-selling the interest rate to a higher interest rate than the flat no commissions paid rate offered by the Lender funding the loan.

That flat rate with no fee paid is referred to as the "par" rate. Sometimes referred to as the "base" rate. More often referred to as Yield Spread Premium (YSP).

As the broker sells a higher rate above the par rate to their borrower, an extra commission incentive is paid to the Broker. This is called par plus.

At "par" the Broker is not paid a fee.

For example: Say 6% is the par rate on a given day. A borrower paying 6.25% earns the broker a par plus fee of 0.5% and at 6.5% earns the broker a par plus fee of 1%.

Par Plus fees are based on the loan amount. On a $100,000 loan a 0.5% fee is $5,00 and 1% fee is $1,000.

Broker greed was typically limited by Private Label Lenders. 3% in prime and 5% in sub-prime. The actual rate was determined by what the willing borrower would pay, whether they shopped around and the selling ability of the broker to get borrowers to pay higher rates.

So a broker could conceivably earn $3,000 to $5,000 on every $100,000 of loan amount with the Par Plus system. Borrowers that didn't qualify for a bank loan were open to broker loan manipulation.

Brokers are required to disclose Par Plus or YSP on the Good Faith Estimate and HUD-1. Lenders are not. This gives lender's an advantage. Lenders can build the par plus into the rate and not disclose it. Calculating the par plus when shopping around is complex for the typical borrower.

Chapter 9

Warehouse Lines of Credit and Warehousing in Private Label MBS

Rogues Alliance

Warehouse lenders are typically commercial banks. In the prior chapters we addressed repeal of the Banking Act of 1933 allowing commercial banks to align with investment banks who bought mortgage loans. Hasty shoddy loan origination and warehousing was a significant problem undermining the foundation of MBS Private Label Securitization.

Greedy investment bankers with talons to seize their wealth of investor funds every week by the billions of dollar in MBS deals fueled the hasty and shoddy practices. In the end, borrowers and investors would suffer.

Overview of the program does not reveal its toxic (poisonous) nature. Investment banks in MBS Private Label Securitization work with the Commercial Banks who aggregate and gather mortgage loans up to sell in bulk quantities called "pools" of loans. Acting in this fashion, warehouse lenders can also be referred to as Aggregators or Securitizers. Investment banks and commercial banks can establish specific related entities to perform this accumulation of loans and sale in pools. They often do so under what are called "flow" agreements. In other words, "we commit to selling you the following flow of loans we originate". When warehouse lender's store up individual loans in this manner they are "Warehousing".

Hasty improperly conducted Warehousing established defective ownership in the chain. Warehouse lending remains a key component of MBS Private Label Trust investors receiving defective loan ownership documentation on loans they purchased in pools. In real estate and mortgage financing, proper evidence of ownership is critical.

Faulty warehousing quality control now causes manufactured documentation in wrongful foreclosure. Borrower's facing wrongful foreclosure continue to come up against Default Loan Servicers who 'manufacture' "proper" loan origination and ownership documents at or around the time of foreclosure. They use a process called "reverse engineering" to present documents in foreclose that were not the documents received by the MBS Securitized Trust of investors when they originally purchased their pool of loans.

Warehouse Lines of Credit were and are used in MBS Private Label Securitization. In GSE MBS Securitization the GSEs funded the loans themselves directly at or near the closing by a wire of funds to the title company or closing agent. There was no need for the originating lender to obtain interim warehouse funding.

Commercial bank Warehouse Lines of Credit provided interim Bridge Funding. In MBS Private Label Securitization it could be days or weeks between the time a borrower closed on their obtaining a loan and the date the eventual MBS Securitization Trust investors closed and paid for the loans they acquired. For this reason commercial banks provided interim "bridge style" temporary funding called "Warehouse Lines of Credit" to originating mortgage bankers.

There is a distinct difference between using or offering a warehouse line of credit and warehousing. The "warehouse line of credit" funds individual mortgage loans. The act of "warehousing" facilitates commercial banks or their entities in accumulating or "aggregating" bulk quantities of individual loans for eventual sale to investment bank's investors.

Flow Agreements

A mortgage banker can enter into an agreement with a commercial bank to "flow" loans to them. The warehouse lender provides warehouse line of credit funds to the mortgage banker so they can close and fund loans. The mortgage banker (lender) provides a steady "flow" of new loans to the warehouse lender so they can aggregate pools of loans to fuel MBS Private Label Securitization.

Warehouse lender funds the mortgage banker's loan to the borrower at closing. At closing the borrower receives that money, usually via a title company or real estate closing attorney by wired funds. If a refinance those parties send off payment on the underlying and if anything left over, such as in a cash out refinance, the borrower is paid minus any fees and expenses paid in the transaction. At this point the warehouse lender's money is gone.

Warehouse lender requires security for lending

Warehouse lenders are savvy commercial banks. They are not going to lend many millions of dollars without security and confirmation of proper documentation in the loan origination process.

Warehouse lender takes ownership of the mortgage loan

The warehouse lender is the initial investor on the loan. Essentially the first buyer of the loan in the eventual chain of buyers along the way to the MBS Private Label Securitization. As the first purchaser, warehouse lenders require receipt of the original loan borrower signed closing documents, with the note properly endorsed.

The mortgage or deed of trust was required to be but in many cases was not properly recorded. MERS, the Mortgage Electronic Registration System was often designated to act as nominee for the Lender in recording the security of the mortgage on and off the county property records. MERS actions were performed by employees of lenders and servicers. MERS is also at the root of wrongful foreclosure and will be covered in more detail in MERS, Chapter 16.

Let's run through a typical warehouse lending scenario.

Here are general steps in the process:

Nitty Gritty of MBS © 2016 Richard M. Kahn

1. The loan is closed in the name of the mortgage banker.

2. The borrower signs the original note and m/dot in "blue ink".

3. The mortgage banker properly endorses the note and assigns the mortgage to the warehouse lender.

4. The title company properly records the Mortgage or Deed of Trust assignment and delivers the document package to the warehouse lender . Notes are endorsed and they are not recorded.

5. The warehouse lender accepts the delivery and optionally files the UCC-1 Financing Statement in the office of the Secretary of State in the state where the borrower is located.

    a. This is the often required procedure to perfect their interest in the Note(s) which evidences the warehouse lender as the owner of the loan. They are also holder of the Note.

    b. The UCC-1 is secured by the Mortgage / Deed of Trust and together they notify the public that the secured party is first in line and first in time with priority interest.

    c. Warehouse lenders are not obligated by law to do this unless they are mandated by a regulatory agency or corporate governance to do so. They may do this to protect their security interest in the loan.

Nitty Gritty of MBS © 2016 Richard M. Kahn

d. The UCC-1 is a form, it is not an agreement of any sort. It is notice to the public of a lien that is created.

e. UCC is an abbreviation for the Uniform Commercial Code.

f. The State in which the property is located and recorded will have a fee for UCC filing.

  i. States typically provide UCC filing forms online.

  ii. As an example, please find footnoted links for Florida[5] and New Hampshire[6]. These have been selected at random for your research convenience.

When the loan is sold, the party purchasing pays the warehouse lender. The warehouse lender takes their agreed upon fee including daily interest rate and passes any additional sale proceeds on to the mortgage banker.

Warehouse lines fund nearly the entire loan origination but not all Warehouse lenders typically provide the mortgage banker with most all (for example: 98%) but not *all* of the loan's funding requirement. This is one reason why many mortgage bankers charge loan origination fees, accept par plus (covered in the previous Chapter 8)

---

[5] Florida: http://www.floridaucc.com/UCCWEB/forms.aspx
[6] New Hampshire http://www.sos.nh.gov/

Nitty Gritty of MBS © 2016 Richard M. Kahn

to cover the spread (for example: 2%) as well as to produce profits in the form of fees for loan origination.

Warehouse lenders offer online computer access to reporting. Computer technology enables ready online access to the daily status of warehouse lines of credit, in much the same fashion as banks provide online statements in the private sector.

Warehouse lenders may put an interim loan number on the loan documents. In examining Notes and Mortgages we often find a number set printed on the face of the documents with no apparent description of what the numbers represent. It is quite possible the numbers represent a warehouse lender's loan number for the subject loan that is entirely different from the originator's loan number.

Warehouse online lender statements may reference multiple loan numbers. In an online warehouse line of credit statement, the mortgage banker can reference their individual loans by both their own loan number and the warehouse lender's loan number.

Warehouse lenders examine funded loan documentation and put in two categories: "Wet" loan or "Dry" Loan. These two are the opposite of Wet Funding settlement and Dry Funding settlement addressed in the prior Chapter 8 (Private Label Table Funding and Par Plus).

The "Wet" Loan

This is an area where loans can become defective due to documentation and recordation problems. Warehouse agreements can and often do allow funding the loan before the warehouse lender receives the full completed original loan documentation package.

That completed loan package includes the loan ownership documentation signed by the borrower at closing. Such as the original Note and Mortgage, supporting documentation, final appraisal and confirmation of required signed disclosures.

When the loan closes at the title company and the borrower receives their funds, this loan is commonly referred to as being in a "Wet Status". Warehouse Lenders designate the length of time, such as ten calendar days, that a loan can be "wet".

The "Dry" Loan

The mortgage banker originating the loan and the title company working with them have a fixed period of time to send the completed loan document package, properly signed, notarized and recorded, to the Warehouse Lender. If all the documentation and underwriting criteria are satisfied it's referred to as a "dry" loan.

You can think of it as getting out of a shower on the way to going to a sale event. If you're wet, you are *not* ready to go out and present yourself. If you're dry, you're ready to go.

"Warehousing" creates an inventory of funded loans that are held in the 'for sale' portfolio.

The MBS Private Label securitized trust buys mortgage pools containing many loans. A typical single MBS mortgage loan pool purchase may include 1,000 to 4,000 loans. It is not uncommon to see single MBS multi-billion dollar mortgage pools containing 7,000 or more loans.

Annual report financial statements can designate these activities in "mortgages held for sale" or "loans held for sale" line items. These activities can include warehousing of purchased loans as well as originated loans that underwent the same process, if the warehouse lender also has wholesale and/or retail loan origination operations.

The loans earmarked for sale are held until the full number of loans and loan amounts required by the specified MBS Private Label Securitization can be provided.

Initial identifications of loans for sale are not schedules of consummated loan sales. Publically traded MBS Private Label Securitization requires disclosures to be filed with the Securities and Exchange Commission (SEC).

Among the documentation filed there may be a preliminary schedule of loans *initially* identified for purchase. This file may be entitled "forward writing prospectus" ("FWP") or "loan tape" and may contain a disclaimer that these are not acquired loans, they are identified loans. There is a big difference. Identified does not mean the loan was acquired, it means these loans are offered for consideration of acquisition. Offers from a commercial lender, authorized intermediary or warehousing pool of loans aggregated for the purpose of sale. Authorized intermediaries can include the bankruptcy remote entities; SPE, QSPE and SPV. (Covered in detail, in Chapter 7 Private Label MBS Securitization).

Here is an analogy: Lists of items on a wedding registry are not gifted items. Do not presume that a loan listed as available in an initial SEC filed preliminary filing document results in that particular warehoused loan being purchased by that particular MBS pool. The typical free writing prospectus will warn of this reality.

Evidence of loan acquisition is in payment, delivery, acceptance and acknowledgement with receipt. The MBS Private Label Securitization deal documents will specify the endorsements and parties in the chain of sales and purchases, from origination to acquisition by the MBS Private Label Securitization Trust.

> Close examination of the Note with endorsements and any Assignments of Mortgage should be performed to confirm actual individual mortgage loan acquisitions by the MBS Private Label Securitization Trust.

"Wet" not ready to go out loans extend warehousing hold times. Loans may experience extended warehousing hold times in the process of a lender completing documentation on a "wet" loan (not ready to go out yet) and requiring time to do so. This may include performing tasks such as ensuring proper endorsement, recordation and making sure all the specific borrower documentation required in the origination, underwriting and compliance with disclosures are present. When that occurs, the loan is "dry" (ready to go out) .

Warehousing is a specific cause of loan documentation defects. Investment banks created tremendous demand from their global clients with money to invest. They put tremendous pressure on the commercial bank's warehousing operations to acquire and turn over their inventory of loans quickly and constantly.

At the heart of the problem, selling "wet" loans before they were "dry" and ready to go. Properly completed and recorded individual mortgage documentation procedure was often compromised for speed of releasing the loan out of warehouse to the investor. In other words, warehouse lenders were not just delivering "dry" ready to go loans, they were delivering "wet" not ready to go loans.

This was a big mistake and the banks knew it. The marriage of commercial banks and investment banks created by repealing the Banking Act of 1933 opened the Pandora's box of greed and manipulation of investor's fortunes. Mortgages just became the vehicle. The problem of haste and greed could be enhanced by either side in this ongoing banking relationship. There was always more investment banker investor money available than commercial bank warehoused "dry" ready to go loans AND "wet" not ready to go loans. Those were the $1x. It was investment bankers that took it to the $8x.

MBS Securitizers selling "wet" loans took improper advantage of REMIC clean up time allowances. Legislative IRS Tax Code in the Real Estate Mortgage Investment Conduit (REMIC) Rules provided time to clean up any documentation. This will be covered in more detail in REMIC Chapter 20.

REMIC 90 day "clean up" rules weren't set up to clear "wet" not ready to go loans. They were designed to allow a MBS Trust's Trustee to go over the thousands of loans the MBS Trust purchased and cull or substitute defective "wet" not ready to go loans.

Buying "wet" not ready to go loans technically undermines ownership of a real estate mortgage. In the real world, an investor or their Trustee would never put up all the money in cash ahead of making sure all the real estate and mortgage financing in the purchase of a mortgage loan was done properly. Settlement and funding of originated loans would not occur absent the proper documentation and recording. Yet in MBS Securitizations, Trustees allowed this. We covered aspects of this risky phenomenon in Chapter 4, Evaluating Ponzi Characteristics of the Mortgage Crisis.

This was not just a problem for MBS Private Label Securitizations. It applies as well to GSE Fannie Mae and Freddie Mac. They too entrusted the Mortgage Banks who often retained documents, to have complete documentation. They also relied on originating lender's representations and warranties to repurchase defective loans, including document errors. The failure to repurchase is a big reason the GSE's failed and are now in Conservatorship. More detail in the next Chapter 10, Agency GSE Securitization, Fannie Mae - Freddie Mac.

The investment bankers and GSEs were so good at their job influencing their investors that the investors were willing to buy intangible mortgage loan assets which in many cases were "wet" and not ready to go. Once the loans were bought and paid for in that status, it became logistically impossible to fix after the fact. Too many new loans needed to be originated and shoved out the door.

➢ In mortgage loan transactions this translates to questionable ownership and clouded chain of title.

Anticipating this beforehand, the banks created MERS to bypass the need to record mortgage assignments in local county property records. This will be covered in the MERS Chapter 16.

➢ Investigating MERS issues are important in litigated foreclosure cases.

Time is money in banking. It costs money to warehouse loans. The object is to minimize the time loans remain warehoused. The faster the loans sell out of the warehouse, the less it costs to keep them and the more is earned.

Another root problem: MBS Investors relied on attestations not on confirmation of "dry" loan receipt. MBS Investors relied on legal and accounting firm attestations and confirmations of proper documentation and recording by reliable firms whose reputation was beyond reproach. The commercial and investment bankers arranged to hire these firms and have them make the necessary attestations. It is easy to see the conflict of interest in that approach. The parties attesting were paid by the Sellers and MBS Trustee who were putting the deals together and selling them to investors.

Neither the parties attesting or the Investors themselves relying on the attestations are were set up to review thousands of loan documents.

Haste of selling "wet" not ready to go loans enabled documentary and recording errors. In mortgage lending these critical areas to prove ownership in cases where default occurred and foreclosure actions were necessary. This is error MBS Securitization lending made which Traditional Lending in the past did not make. The reason being, Traditional Lenders knew that proper documentation and recording was necessary to foreclose on the debt if and when it went into default.

Investors disregarded a cardinal rule.
They paid MBS Securitization lenders in full before ALL the mortgage loans they purchased were "dry" and ready to go.

> ➤ In real estate mortgage ownership, this is a big "no no" because it can challenge the right to foreclose when and if loans default.

Robo-signing and reverse engineering of loan ownership documentation. Trying to correct the old problems at the time of a foreclosure results in such toxic findings as back dating, robo-signing and document fabrication.

> ➤ Areas for a mortgage foreclosure fraud investigator to expose.

Examination of properly maintained warehouse aging reports can identify specific loans and detail of how long they were warehoused. Other factors should also be ascertainable, such as why a particular loan or loans were held on to for more than the average release period.

Warehouse executive management greed

Dealing with tens of thousands of loans requires proper management of warehousing operations to insure loans are not maintained for extended periods. Bank executives typically enjoy generous bonuses, in addition to job security, for timely turnover. This contributes to the phenomenon of selling "wet" loans before they were ready to go.

Keeping loans warehoused for extended periods is not always a losing proposition. When the interest rate being paid by the borrower on the loan is more than the cost to borrow money to carry the loan on the books, this positive spread results in profits.

For example: a borrower is paying 8% and the cost to warehouse the loans is 5%, there is a 3% positive spread. That's a 60% profit over the course of one year. Considering that a warehouse portfolio may include tens of thousands of loans, a spread like that can be quite enriching.

To illustrate: $2 billion of warehoused loans held in the "loans held for sale" portfolio with a 3% positive spread yields $60,000,000 (sixty million dollars) a year, or $5 million a month.

Warehouse operations are comparatively small. They can operate in a tidy suite of "off the beaten track" offices. No retail or distribution locations necessary. A billion dollars of mortgage loan ownership documents can be in a tidy group of easily transported boxes and fit into a van.

Warehouse Aggregators "hedge" their costs of maintaining warehouse loans. Managing business risks, costs of maintaining warehouse lines of credit and inventory of loans is a complex undertaking that requires understanding and ability. Warehouse Aggregators hedge to insure themselves from losses. Hedges can take a trading position in the marketplace that balances the risks assumed in the business. As time passes, the costs of maintaining these interest rate hedge positions can erode profitability.

The objective of Warehousing is fast in and out loan flow. In practice, the faster the loans are sold, the more profitable the loan warehouse transaction is to the seller and aggregator. Loans on which sale is delayed for longer periods of time than planned indicate problems. Problems manifest themselves in various ways. Lingering delays likely indicate significant defects that can be included in segments such as underwriting deficiencies, defaulted loan payments, interests that are below what is saleable to investors, documentation, recordation and any other problem which affects the ability to sell a particular loan to an investor. In the process of balancing the business risk, "wet" not ready to go loans were allowed to slip out in sales to MBS.

Foreclosure on loans owned by MBS protects the sellers of those loans from financial risk. Foreclosure after the MBS has purchased loans, severs the business risk of passing defective loans sold "without recourse" and cancels the repurchase agreement. In other words the investors cannot force a repurchase once a foreclosure has removed a loan from the MBS Trust pool.

The original warehouse transaction had a paper trail in the form of Aging Reports. Regulatory agencies can require banks, such as savings and thrifts, regulated by the Office of Thrift Supervision (OTS) in the years prior to mortgage meltdown 2008, to maintain warehouse aging reports.

In discovery, one target can be the general ledger of a Warehouse Lender. Generally Accepted Accounting Principles (GAAP) require warehouse lenders maintain these ledgers. Banks may be required by their regulators to comply. For example, savings and loan thrift institutions are required to maintain general ledgers to enter and reconcile warehouse loan activities.

It is standard policy for banks and financial institutions to monitor and reconcile warehouse line ledgers *daily*.

The fundamental issues of warehouse accounting and hedging can be very complex. Upper management designate qualified individuals or committees to manage warehouse risk exposure, monitor and manage their pipeline to identify risk as soon as possible and routinely assess the situations.

It is customary for these risk management personnel to provide periodic reporting and you will find reference to this in many banking entity annual reports. In addition you will find reporting on the hedging and risk aversion products utilized in the process.

To significantly lessen the complex accounting required in the hedging process many entities 'fair value' these activities.

To recap the warehousing process:
1. The mortgage banker originates a loan to a borrower or borrowers.

Nitty Gritty of MBS © 2016 Richard M. Kahn

2. The mortgage banker obtains funding from their warehouse line to fund the loan at closing. The borrower(s) close. The loan is now in "wet status". The mortgage banker assigns the Note and Mortgage to the warehouse lender as security.

3. During "wet status" period, the mortgage banker and title company have a prescribed time by the warehouse lender to cure any deficiencies in the loan documentation. For example, one week or ten days.

4. The mortgage banker already knows to whom they are selling the loan in the investor secondary market. This may be a MBS trust or an aggregator of loans who intends to sell to an MBS. The transactions may take place under a Flow Agreement.

5. There are different methods to sell loans. Whole loan sales can be done on the face value of the loan amount evidenced by the Note. Cash flow sales are based on yield spreads and include calculations for interest strips that have been retained. Warehouse transactions are typically done on the whole loan sales amounts, leaving cash flow sales profits to the aggregator to perform apart from the warehouse transaction.

Chapter 10

Agency GSE Securitization[7]

Fannie Mae - Freddie Mac

The Government Sponsored Enterprises (GSEs) include the Federal National Mortgage Association, more commonly known as "Fannie Mae" and abbreviated "FNMA" and also the Federal Home Loan Mortgage Corporation, more commonly known as "Freddie Mac" and abbreviated "FHLMC".

The types of GSE guidelines addressed here are those which generally apply to the origination years 2000 through 2008. Since the mortgage meltdown and financial crisis things have changed. It is important to reference the guidelines that existed both at loan origination as well

---

[7] Some information may have been gathered and confirmed from the government sponsored enterprise program's web site or publications.

as those existing at time of foreclosure. This is made all the more difficult for the non-expert considering the GSEs are updating their guides and making announcements regularly.

Both Fannie Mae and Freddie Mac have their own specific sales, servicing and document custody guidelines. These include all the areas of activity for mortgage loans. There are sections for all conceivable actions including default loan servicing and loan modification requirements. The guides are thousands of pages and revised regularly. Links to all documentation are available on their web sites.

An expert knows how to navigate the complexities of the GSE guidelines and updates. This may be difficult for those who are uninitiated.

> The key to making a contested foreclosure case in GSE MBS securitizations lies in familiarity with the requirements and guidelines of the GSEs. These cases are made quite differently than the Private Label Securitizations and SPE Bank to Bank securitizations.

GSE Securitization involves fewer true sales and skips the bankruptcy remote SPV financial engineering and credit enhancement phases of the Private Label Securitization model described in Chapter 7. GSE Securitization employs many other common elements of Securitization including the Document Custodian and True Sales aspects of the securitization model.

The GSEs give their approved loan sellers, servicers and document custodians a lot of leeway in terms of rights and authority to act on behalf of the GSEs in selling, servicing , document custody and foreclosure.

Borrower signs Note and Mortgage with Originator; then loan docs to Document Custodian on True Sale to GSE Fannie Mae or Freddie Mac; who turns the mortgages into securities, placing their own corporate guaranty on interest payments for sale of Certificates to investors.

Freddie Mac is modeled similarly to Fannie Mae, so for illustration purposes references to Fannie Mae include Freddie Mac unless otherwise noted.

Fannie Mae offers two primary ways lenders transact business. Selling whole loans for cash and pooling loans into Fannie Mae mortgage backed securities (MBS). The Selling, Servicing and Document Custody guides include policies and procedures that pertain to both execution options.

Selling Whole Loans to Fannie Mae

Fannie Mae provides several methods for lenders to sell whole loans to Fannie Mae. These may be mandatory, best efforts or converted ARM resale commitments. In each, lenders are paid in cash for the loans sold when the lender has delivered the mortgages, once all Fannie Mae underwriting and legal criteria have been met. Fannie Mae refers to this as "good delivery".

Original Mortgage Loan Documentation Delivery is made to Fannie Mae's Designated Document Custodian ("DDC") by overnight carrier the same day the seller submits the loan data to Fannie Mae for purchase. The DDC reviews the related mortgage documentation to verify that all required documents are received and are in order. Any deficiencies are reported to the lender who works with the DDC to resolve any document issues. Upon confirmation of a clean error-free loan delivery the lender is paid in full for the mortgage loan amount plus profit.

Nitty Gritty of MBS © 2016 Richard M. Kahn

Pooling Whole Loans into Fannie Mae MBS

To enable Lenders to sell Fannie Mae pools of loans that have similar characteristics, Lenders obtain pool purchase contracts with varying terms.

"Fannie Mae MBS" and "Fannie Mae MBS Securitizations" are synonymous. The two terms are exactly the same and interchangeable. In the Private Label Securitizations we used the word "securitizations" extensively. When referring to GSE MBS securitizations in this book we will refer to them as GSE MBS or MBS.

Fannie Mae issues an MBS backed by the loans in one of two transaction types.

- "Swap and Hold": the lender holds the securitized MBS certificates after the MBS is created. The lender is then the investor as well as the seller.

- "Swap and Sell": the securitized MBS certificates are immediately sold to other investors.

Lenders sell a wide variety of loans to Fannie Mae in two basic ways: for cash, or securitization via a bulk transaction. Fannie Mae provides a Capital Markets Sales Desk to facilitate this. Whole loans are sold at a "live" price that fluctuates with the MBS market throughout any given day.

Fannie Mae MBS are known as "pass through certificates" because the interest and principal on the underlying mortgages in the pool are passed through to investors without the double taxation of a corporation.

Fannie Mae guarantees that the related mortgages held by a particular trust will receive timely payments of principal and interest. In the event of a shortfall, Fannie Mae will supplement underpayments. In exchange for this guarantee, Fannie Mae receives fees.

Fannie Mae MBS provide varying types of ownership:

- <u>Fractional</u>, meaning less than a whole loan amount;

- <u>Undivided</u>, meaning a whole loan amount; and

- <u>Beneficial interests</u> in a particular designated distinct pool of mortgages. These may include conventional non-government insured or guaranteed loans, government insured FHA, government guaranteed VA and HUD guaranteed loans.

There are two types of Fannie Mae MBS pools.

- A **single lender pool** where all the mortgages are similar in a common characteristic, such as loan type (fixed, adjustable) or amortization (15 year, 30 year), et cetera.

- **Fannie Majors**: A multiple lender pool consisting of whole mortgages delivered by more than one lender.

In GSE MBS trust pools of single family loans, Fannie Me buys the loans from one or more lenders and issues Fannie Mae MBS backed by those particular mortgages. In this capacity Fannie Mae acts as Trustee in its corporate capacity under a Trust Agreement. Fannie Mae posts the individual single family master trust agreements for the specific issuances on its web site.

Fannie Mae establishes "seasoning" requirements that limit the age since origination of a loan. For example, conventional loans in each pool have generally been originated within the last 12 months of the GSE MBS issue date. Hybrid ARMs adjust their rate annually after their extended initial fixed interest rate periods, cannot be seasoned more than two months as of the pool issue date.

- ➢ This seasoning is a critical defect issue in many contested foreclosure litigations where an Agency GSE is involved and the chain of title has been falsified.

➤ We often find faulty assignments to Fannie Mae or Freddie Mac. For instance, made after 12 months on conventional loans; and after 2 months on Hybrid ARMS.

Hybrid ARMS blend characteristics of fixed rate loans with those of adjustable rate loans. The initial fixed rate period is followed by an adjustable rate. For example: ten years fixed, then adjustable. Once the fixed rate term is reached, the loan begins to adjust based upon the margin specified added to the Index specified. An index is an accessible rate such as the Wall Street Journal or a newspaper published in an easily accessible venue.

Fannie Mae does not service the loans. Technically the GSEs are the Owner/Holder/Master Servicers with the rights as owners to service but in practice the actual day to day loan servicing responsibility falls to the selling lender who receives compensation for it in the process. While it may be a little confusing, this designated selling lender is actually considered the Holder/Master Servicer. But they are not the "owner". Fannie Mae remains the owner on all loans they acquire.

The Holder/Master Servicer has the right to designate sub-servicing of day to day loan servicing but remains wholly responsible for the Master Servicing performance according to the Servicing Guidelines.

- Going forward the GSE selling lender is referred to as the Master Servicer or just Servicer.

➢ Claims in a questionable foreclosure that the loan is actually serviced by Fannie Mae or any Agency GSE "themselves are unfounded. Fannie Mae does not actually perform the day to day loan servicing on loans it owns.

Guaranty Fee

For the service of allowing others to perform loan servicing, Fannie Mae charges a fee; called a guaranty fee. It is not based on mortgage pool cash flows. The fee is a responsibility of the lender and the fee is due even if no collections are made on the underlying obligations.

Each mortgage is included in a Purchase Advice identified by a Fannie Mae loan number. The selling lender, now called the Master Servicer or simply Servicer, must enter the Fannie Mae loan number into their records immediately and all subsequent activity is tagged to the loan number.

Lenders must select an eligible Document Custodian and have an executed Master Custodial Agreement signed before Fannie Mae will purchase and pay for pooled loans. The document custodian takes in, certifies and retains actual possession of the properly endorsed and assigned loan documents for each mortgage. Document custodians must meet strict custodian eligibility criteria. Fannie Mae may also provide their Designated Document Custodian (DDC) for MBS loans.

There are two types of servicing options that impact Fannie Mae guaranty fees.

- **The <u>Regular Servicing Option</u>** incurs a lower fee. Here the lender, now the servicer, assumes the entire risk of loss from a borrower defaulting on a loan while the servicer is servicing that mortgage. The lender agrees that when and if they sell the loan servicing, the successor servicer will also be legally bound and agree to assume this liability.

  The entire risk of loss to the lender once they become the servicing lender, refers to the servicing lender's unrecovered advances for borrower mortgage payment delinquencies and advances related to servicing the mortgages.

- Fannie Mae pays the lender in full for the face value of the mortgage at the time Fannie Mae purchases the loan from the lender.

- **The Special Servicing Option** finds Fannie Mae assuming the risk of loss from borrower default on a loan. Again, risk of loss is to the servicing lender's unrecovered advances for delinquencies and advances related to servicing the mortgages.

Note Endorsement

The originating lender must be the original payee on the note, even when the Mortgage Electronic Registration System (MERS) is named as nominee for the beneficiary in the mortgage security instrument. MERS will be addressed in further detail in MERS - Tool of Deception, Chapter 16.

- The note must be endorsed to each subsequent owner of the mortgage unless one or more of the owners endorsed the note in *blank*; meaning pay to the order of _____.
- The last endorsement on the note should be that of the mortgage seller selling to Fannie Mae.
- The mortgage seller must endorse the note in blank and without recourse.
- The endorsement must appear on the note.
- An allonge or attached piece of paper permanently affixed to the note, clearly identifying the note. The allonge must

comply with all applicable state laws (see below for more detail on allonges).

- Fannie Mae's status as "holder in due course" must not be impaired.

Allonge

For those unfamiliar with the term "allonge", it's a signature page permanently attached to a Note.

- Quoting from Black's Law Dictionary (4th ed. 1951) page 100:, defines *"allonge" as "[a] piece of paper annexed to a bill of exchange or promissory note, on which to write endorsements for which there is no room on the instrument itself." Webster's Third New International Dictionary (1964) page 57, gives a similar definition: "a slip of paper attached to a bill of exchange or similar document to provide space for additional endorsements."*

States often carry definitions of "Allonge" cited within their State Appellate Decisions which may appear as a footnote ("FN") to the decision.

The Author does not cite legalities as he is not an attorney. The author is a testifying expert. Experts, unless they are attorneys, do not cite legal issues, especially in their reporting.

- That said, and simply to illustrate one example where the definition of an Allonge may be found in a decision, and not to provide any legal commentary whatsoever on the issue, the definition of Allonge used above is taken from one of California's footnoted definitions of Allonge in a court case. It was referenced as FN 6 in Pribus v. Bush, Civ. No. 23473, Court of Appeal of California, Fourth Appellate District, Division Two, 118 Cal. App. 3d 1003; 173 Cal. Rptr. 747; 1981 Cal. App. LEXIS 1724; 31 U.C.C. Rep. Serv. (Callaghan) 599, May 12, 1981

Fannie Mae is always the holder and owner of the Note. The original loan documents on loans purchased by Fannie Mae are given to the Document Custodian who abides by the official Document Custodian Protocol. Basically that translates to putting the file boxes of valuable original holder in due course endorsed Notes and assigned Mortgages into the Document Custodian's qualifying vaults.

A critical element of transfer is that the selling lender indemnifies Fannie Mae from any loss as a result of improper note endorsement. This means repurchase when and if defects are discovered on a particular loan. For example, defects can include in conveyance, recording and underwriting standards.

MERS

Lenders must prepare assignments of mortgage if the mortgage is not registered with MERS but the assignments are not required to be recorded when the loan is sold to Fannie Mae.

- The unrecorded assignments are delivered to Fannie Mae in executed form by the lender servicer. Fannie Mae provides standard forms for this purpose.

- The assignee is Fannie Mae, "without recourse" and must be prepared in recordable form.

- MERS will be addressed in further detail in MERS - Tool of Deception, Chapter 16.

Fannie Mae allows lenders to use MERS with specific understandings:

- Even though MERS is named as the nominee for the beneficiary in the security instrument, MERS has no beneficial ownership interest in the mortgage.

- If a lender uses MERS to register a mortgage before selling to Fannie Mae the mortgage identification number ("MIN") must appear on the loan and the loan schedule.

- Before Fannie Mae purchases, the lender must notify MERS about Fannie Mae's ownership.

- After Fannie Mae purchases or securitizes the mortgage, Fannie Mae notifies MERS of Fannie Mae's ownership interest.

MERS registration of the mortgage facilitates data entry recording by the current loan servicer. The MERS authorized representative is an employee of the MERS member; an employee of the lender seller and/or the subsequent loan servicer. The loan servicer by its employee authorized for MERS access, can change the MERS records via computer connected to the Internet. Fannie Mae therefore is specific that if the servicing lender is going to use MERS, MERS as nominee must be indicated on the mortgage security instrument and related documents.

MERS Assignments do NOT include the Note

When an originating lender retains a beneficial interest in the mortgage on a mortgage that is registered with MERS as nominee for the beneficial owner, the servicing lender must prepare an assignment of the mortgage to MERS. This is not an assignment of the Note. Notes are not assigned, they are endorsed.

Loan servicing retained or released. When lenders sell loans to Fannie Mae, they designate whether they will retain loan servicing or release loan servicing to another servicer approved by Fannie Mae.

Wiring funds to pay for loans vs. issuing securities

On whole loan transactions where Fannie Mae purchases the loans, it wires funds to the lender at purchase. For MBS pooled loans, Fannie Mae issues securities to the lender which the lender may hold in their portfolio or sell; or designate be delivered to the investor directly by Fannie Mae.

Loan data for all of the purchased mortgages must be sent electronically to Fannie Mae using Loan Delivery for either MBS mortgages or whole loan deliveries.

Fannie Mae has Quality Control (QC) requirements. These require, among other things, that a servicing lender maintain documentation as well as arrangements with the subservicers which allow full access to any loan files transferred; so the assigning lender can perform QC. **Every loan sold to Fannie Mae is designated to be an unconditional sale to Fannie Mae** of all rights, title and interest. Lenders are required to indemnify Fannie Mae for breaches by a lender to satisfy its duties and responsibilities in the process. Repurchase of the loan is

Nitty Gritty of MBS © 2016 Richard M. Kahn

another possibility, as is Substitution of a different acceptable loan within allowable time frames and parameters Fannie Mae designates in their published Selling Guides.

Fannie Mae issues MBS and Stripped MBS ("SMBS"). "Stripped" means separating the principal payments and interest payments from the underlying mortgages. One investor may receive Interest Only ("IO"), another Investor might receive Principal Only ("PO"), or different classes of certificates may receive different portions of each.

Certificates are not always issued on new mortgages. They are often issued on previously issued certificates from other trusts and other mortgage related assets such as the SMBS mentioned.

> ➤ This is or should be a grave cause of concern to anyone evaluating exactly what piece of property security interest is owned by a particular investor. New money came in for the initial trust that owned the property interest ($1x). By purchasing new certificates in previously issued MBS, that security interest is diluted each time the process occurs ($2x, $3x, etc).

> ➤ In other words, the underlying loan(s) represented in one set of issued certificates of a new MBS is really essentially being

secured by a prior original mortgaged property sold as security for a prior issued MBS.

➢ Translated: one particular mortgage security is being sold over and over again when this occurs. This highly toxic phenomenon makes GSE MBS similar in nature to the $1x to $8x selling and reselling of individual mortgage loans by Private Label MBS addressed in earlier chapters. It continues to escalate in seriousness.

➢ For these reasons, it is essential to require production of the properly perfected loan ownership documentation of Notes and Mortgages in Agency GSE securitizations. It is also pertinent to request discovery revealing how many times and to which additional MBS trusts a particular mortgage was sold and resold.

GSE MBS echoing the Ponzi scheme aspect of Private Label Securitizations. In Fannie Mae and Freddie Mac Agency GSE securitizations we find the GSE corporations themselves selling the loan over and over again.

- In both cases, the profit is reaped not by the borrowers, but by those GSEs securitizing the loans.

- The borrower provides the product and the investor provides the money, presumably for new loans.
- In the case of GSEs reselling certificates already secured by previously sold loans, the GSEs are reaping windfall profits of incoming dollars that were not used to buy new loans; the dollars bought diluted security interests in existing loans.
- It is the basis of a continuing Ponzi scheme activity delineated in Chapter 4, Evaluating Ponzi Characteristics o the Mortgage Crisis. Fannie Mae continues this reselling of past issuances, taking in new principal dollars against a $1x loan, promising to pay interest on it and keeping the principal.

All Agency GSE mortgage purchase transactions include Document Custodianship and there is an established paper trail required for each loan.

> Discovery should be directed if there is a question of authenticity.

There are no Pooling and Servicing Agreements in GSE MBS transactions. There is also no "Depositor" as there is in the Private Label Securitization model. The Depositor function in the Private Label model is/was to create a "bankruptcy remote" insulation factor the investors require to insure the loan assets they are purchasing actually belong to them in case of bankruptcy by any party in the prior chain of sale process.

Fannie Mae and Freddie Mac's implied U.S. Government backing does not exist.

That initial U.S. Government backing provided when Fannie Mae was created, is an implied benefit now, it is not a guarantee by the U.S. Government. It may be thought of as existing but has not existed since Fannie Mae became non-Government owned.

Fannie Mae became a corporation around 1970 and initially traded on the NYSE. Investors do not receive and no longer require that U.S. Government guaranty insulation. As previously stated, interest and monthly payments are guaranteed by Fannie Mae and Freddie Mac, the corporations. Fannie Mae and Freddie Mac are backed by hundreds of billions of dollars of infusions by the U.S. Government. Paid for by U.S. Taxpayers. Their stocks are pennies on the dollar and they have been in conservatorship since the collapse of financial markets and the mortgage meltdown in 2008.

Too Big to Fail

From US Government actions, continuing to dump vast sums into Fannie Mae and Freddie Mac under their conservatorship, we can see that Fannie Mae and Freddie Mac are considered "too big to fail". We hear the topic of dissolution discussed from time to time.

The Fed and U.S. Treasury are and have been pumping hundreds of billions of taxpayer dollars into both entities to prop them up, even while these GSE entity's stock prices have fallen so low that both GSEs were delisted from the New York Stock Exchange. Both companies found their stock, once high flying darlings, trading for pennies per share.

On September 7, 2008 the Director of the Federal Housing Finance Agency (FHFA is the regulator and conservator of Fannie Mae and Freddie Mac), and 12 Federal Home Loan Banks, put Fannie Mae and Freddie Mac into conservatorship. As Conservator, FHFA has all rights, powers, title and interest to these Fannie Mae and Freddie Mac corporations and assets.

In the process of contested foreclosure:
- Documentation for Fannie Mae and Freddie Mac MBS transactions are encompassed in the individual deal documents and many thousands of pages of Guides. These are all available to the public online at the GSE web sites. The Guides are revised regularly and a historic access to the

Nitty Gritty of MBS © 2016 Richard M. Kahn

pertinent guide at any given date is provided. It is important to reference the pertinent guide issued at the date of the mortgage origination and/or the loan securitization in question or being investigated.

Claims of ownership by Fannie Mae and Freddie Mac

Both Fannie Mae and Freddie Mac provide individual loan level lookup tools with public access via the Internet. The actual web site address URLs may change. Enter Fannie Mae loan lookup or Freddie Mac loan lookup on your favorite search engine.

Fannie Mae claims their core income comes from guarantee fees.

These fees are paid in exchange for Fannie Mae guaranteeing timely principal and interest payments on fixed rate participation certificates and interest on adjustable rate mortgage certificates.

Hidden source of income and problems

Fannie Mae resells previously securitized mortgage loans without purchasing them from prior issued GSE MBS investors. This leaves Investors and taxpayers at huge risk.

Chapter 11

Fannie, Freddie and the Fed

Building on the prior chapter, we can now proceed to understand the relationship between the GSEs, the U.S. Taxpayer and the Federal Reserve ("Fed") who controls all the money supply in the United States. This relationship continues to expose U.S. Taxpayers with bailing out the GSEs, a tremendous financial burden.

The Federal Reserve is owned by its member banks. The MBS Securitization mortgage loan financial products created were part of their member banks' profit margins. The Fed bolstered and continues to bolster the GSEs purchase and sale of these products with taxpayer dollars collected by the US Treasury.

To keep mortgages from defaulting both for the good of homeowners and to prevent the member banks from losing a huge source of income, the Federal Government has mandated loan workouts be performed by the Government Sponsored Enterprises (Fannie Mae, Freddie Mac, etc.) and member banks.

There is a relationship between the Fed, its member banks and the GSEs. The Fed is the bid daddy of all banks. U.S. Taxpayers are like the hoard upon which the member banks and the government feed.

Venture to say, what many U.S. Taxpayers do not understand is the fact that all Fannie Mae and Freddie Mac GSE interest and principal disbursements to investors clears through the Fed and benefits earnings systematically to the member banks, feeding the member banks earnings on an ongoing basis. This, more than anything else may be what's *really* behind the continued bailouts to the GSEs.

Whenever people spend money in America, a percentage is peeled off for taxes along the way, in addition to purchase taxes which all go to Government. In this same manner, whenever payments are made against the trillions of dollars the GSEs have issued in MBS securitizations, a percentage is peeled off and goes to the Fed and its member banks.

Nitty Gritty of MBS © 2016 Richard M. Kahn

Here is how that **process** works.

Brief recap of GSEs Fannie Mae and Freddie Mac

Federal National Mortgage Association (FNMA or more commonly
Fannie Mae) and the Federal Home Loan Mortgage Corporation
(FHLMC or more commonly Freddie Mac) are Government Sponsored
Enterprises (GSEs). Both are publically traded financial services
corporations currently in Conservatorship and avoiding bankruptcy.
Both continue to soak up hundreds of billions of U.S. Taxpayer dollars
on top of tremendous bailouts paid to banks with little accounting
involved. Fannie Mae was created by Congress. Freddie Mac was
authorized by Congress.

The original GSE idea was to enhance the flow of mortgage credit by
creating a secondary marketplace where investors could purchase
mortgage backed securities (MBS). Regulators and the public believed
Fannie and Freddie's MBS pre-2000 activities were efficient and
transparent. They essentially were.

Fannie Mae and Freddie Mac purchase mortgages from mortgage
originators and mortgage sellers under the Fannie Mae Charter Act.
This establishes requirements and limitations on the mortgages
purchased.

Fannie Mae and Freddie Mac act as the Depositor does in Private Label MBS securitizations. Fannie Mae and Freddie Mac purchase mortgages then transfer and deposit mortgages into various MBS trusts that are established pursuant to written Participation Certificate ("PC") Agreements.

Fannie Mae and Freddie Mac's core income comes from guarantee fees, guaranteeing timely principal and interest payments on fixed rate and adjustable rate mortgage participation certificates (PCs).

Fannie Mae and Freddie Mac act in their corporate capacity as Depositor, Administrator and Guarantor.

To get an understanding of how payments from these GSEs benefit the Fed and its member banks on each and every payment made to the investors, let's examine the features of the Certificates sold to investors. These are the same "Cows in hamburger out" or "Mortgages in Certificates out" characterized by MBS Securitization. Only with a significant "pay interest to the Fed, pay stripped off fees to the member banks" twist. This feature is another that differentiates Private Label MBS Securitization from Agency GSE Securitization.

Participation Certificates (PCs)

Fannie Mae and Freddie Mac purchase mortgages and form PC Pools. The PCs represent an undivided beneficial ownership interest in the assets of the PC Pool. Fannie Mae and Freddie Mac then act as the Trustee for the PC Pool, guaranteeing timely payment of principal and interest for the benefit of the investors who own and hold the PCs. Acting as Administrator, Fannie Mae and Freddie Mac administer the affairs of each PC Pool.

Fannie Mae and Freddie Mac's PC Pools can contain many investments other than mortgages. There are many other eligible investments, other than mortgages that can be included. For example: any obligation of the USA, Agency, instrumentality, State, municipality, local government; time deposits of any institution of trust company domiciled in Nassau or the Cayman Islands as long as they are affiliated with a financial institution that is a member of the Federal Reserve System; federal funds, certificates of deposit, bankers acceptances; commercial paper, debt securities, money market funds and other investment vehicles. including MBS securities insured or guaranteed by an entity that is an agency or instrumentality of the United States.

The assets represented in each pool of issued participation certificates are required to be identified in Fannie Mae and Freddie Mac corporate records.

PC Pools can re-sell mortgages already securitized over and over again For those evaluating the Ponzi scheme aspect of securitization from earlier chapters, this category is ripe for consideration. Fannie Mae has names for these re-sales, such as re-REMICs, Related Combinable and Recombinable ("RCR") classes and Stripped Mortgage Backed Securities ("SMBS"). PC's may contain previously issued certificates in other MBS pools. PC Pools can also contain repurchase obligations, meaning MBS assets subject to repurchase under written agreements.

Raising Ponzi scheme concerns.

WE covered Ponzi characteristics in Chapter 4. Here is additional food for thought. New money coming in from investors but purchasing individually secured mortgage loans on individual properties which have already been sold into other MBS pools. The underlying security for the investment is the certificate that was issued against single unique properties and mortgages, not the single unique property or mortgage loan itself. This continues to be done, over and over.

We had already gone over the $8 trillion in real properties securing MBS securitizations resulting in $62 trillion of sales and MBS securitizations asset valuation in 2008, just prior to the financial collapse. After the collapse that valuation was about $32 trillion. But there are still only $8 trillion of underlying individual properties. So now, instead of $1x for $8x it's $1x for $4x. Still a grave problem.

Purchase Certificates (PCs) are a financial instrument and a form of financing. PCs are funded by investors who buy a share of the assets and revenues in the PC Pool.

As Depositor, Fannie Mae transfers and deposits these Mortgages and issued Participation Certificates in other purchased mortgages into various trust funds formed pursuant to Trust Agreements and Pool Supplements.

Assets in PC Certificates out

Fannie Mae and Freddie Mac act as "Trustee" for the trust funds they create. The assets go in, and Participation Certificates (PCs) come out in the form of stock and bond style ownership with minimum denominations of $1,000; and in $1 increments after that. In the exact same manner as the previous analogy of "cows in, hamburger out", it is difficult (or impossible) for an investor to identify a particular asset or "cow" represented by certificate ownership in the asset once the PC "hamburger" has been issued. The investor simply receives a pro-rata share in the principal and/or receives interest payments as applicable.

Revealing the Federal Reserve's hand in Participation Certificates

The PCs are issued, held and transferable only on the book-entry system of the Federal Reserve banks. Fannie Mae prospectuses memorialize this including specifics, in their book-entry procedures sections.

The ultimate Good old Boy PC Ownership Network

Only banking institutions that are members of the Federal Reserve System may be holders of PCs.

One PC is issued. A designated Depository Trust Company ("DTC") holds the one PC certificate issued in the GSE MBS securitization. The DTC now creates its own Certificate, the DTC Certificate. Financial intermediaries (banks) can own ownership positions in the DTC Certificate. Banks can also be financial intermediaries for investors. The DTC keeps track of the bank ownership positions in the DTC Certificate.

Investors in PCs are not recognized by Fannie Mae on their PC investment. Investors have to rely on the deal they make with their bank. Fannie Mae doesn't recognize investors themselves. Investors have to go through the financial intermediaries (banks) or a Depository Participant (bank) who acts as agent for the financial intermediary. It's the bank with whom the investor has a relationship.

How the Fed and Member Banks get their share of PC distributions

- On each payment date a Federal Reserve Bank credits payments to the account of each Holder on the Federal Reserve Bank's book entry system (bank).
- Each Holder and each financial intermediary in the chain to the actual beneficial owners of the PCs are responsible to remit payments to their Customers, minus a designated spread on the interest paid of course.

Banks buy the PCs with their investor customer's funds.

The bank's Customers are the ones who put up the cash but Fannie Mae and Freddie Mac do not register or monitor that aspect. They only monitor payment to the institutions that are members of the Federal Reserve System (banks) who purchased the PCs with their own or Customer's money.

Nitty Gritty of MBS © 2016 Richard M. Kahn

Swap transaction terms facilitate the arrangement

Fannie Mae and Freddie Mac issue PCs, mostly in guarantee swap transactions to their banking customers. The swap transaction terms facilitate the arrangement where the banks earn fees on participation, funneling the payments from the GSE through to the eventual investing bank customer.

Take Fannie Mae for instance, their top 10 banking customers represented nearly 80% of Fannie Mae's business in 2010. In the guarantee swaps the banks provide the mortgage loans (or other eligible investments as previously listed above).

Fannie Mae and Freddie Mac provide the PCs as administrator of the trusts they establish.

Here's how the GSE banking customers make money on PCs.

The GSEs have sold trillions of dollars of PC issuances in MBS Securitizations and their bank customers earn a spread on those monthly payments.

The GSE spread

Because of Fannie Mae and Freddie Mac's perceived guarantee value, the GSE bank customers (banks) customers (investors) are willing to accept a lower interest rate of return than the individual mortgage borrowers pay on their mortgages. Mortgage payments which are remitted to the GSE's by their loan servicers.

The GSE Bank Customer's spread

The profitably from a bank's point of view, being a Fannie Mae or Freddie Mac "banking customer" is earning a spread on the interest they are receiving and the lower interest they are paying to their own customers (investors).

This process is called "stripping" or "peeling"

This process of capitalizing on interest differentials is called stripping interest or peeling off interest strips. (Detailed in Chapter 18, Interest strips - profits in excess of cash flow).

The money flow

On each payment date a Federal Reserve Bank credits payments to the account of each Holder (bank) on the Federal Reserve Bank's book entry system. Each Holder and each financial intermediary in the chain to the actual beneficial owners of the PCs are responsible to remit payments to their Customers.

With the Federal Reserve Bank making the payments, their member banks are the only ones to know exactly how much is being paid by Fannie Mae under the mortgages.

It's up to the banks to disburse rates of return to their investor customers who purchased the PCs. The banks originated the mortgages at higher interest rates, Fannie Mae and Freddie Mac securitized them, then feed the cash flow back to the banks so that the banks can earn the interest rate spreads as hidden profits.

Let's make some calculation projections to get an idea of the actual numbers we are talking about.

Example: Bank originates a mortgage for $100,000. Let's calculate that the interest rate on the mortgage is 8%. The annual interest the borrower pays is $8,000.

Calculating profits on a single deal size of $1 billion in GSE MBS securitizations

Loan amount markup

Let's assume the bank's investor customers are willing to purchase Fannie Mae and Freddie Mac guaranteed MBS PCs at a 4% return. The bank's investor customers pay $200,000 for the $8,000 cash flow. $8,000/.04 = $200,000. Original loan to borrower was $100,000. GSE MBS Securitization loan amount based on the lower yield required by GSE investors is $200,000.

Loan Amount Markup Profit: $100,000

Estimate GSE MBS deal size = $1 Billion which translates into 10,000 $100,000 units. Multiply $100,000 x 10,000 = $1 billion dollars profit on ONE full GSE MBS Securitization.

Loan Interest stripping markup

In the above example, the mortgage borrower is paying 8% or $8,000 per year. An investor buying GSE AAA rated PC certificates is willing to accept 4%. CD interest for comparison maybe 1.5%.

Receive $8,000 per year, pay $4,000 per year.

Loan Interest stripping markup profit: $4,000 per year

Estimate GSE MBS deal size = $1 Billion which translates into 10,000 $100,000 units. Multiply $4,000 x 10,000 = $40 million dollars profit per year on ONE full GSE MBS Securitization.

(Interest strips - profits in excess of cash flow, is covered in more detail in Chapter 18).

Nitty Gritty of MBS © 2016 Richard M. Kahn

PC interest peeling fee

For the GSE banking customer acting as a financial intermediary to the bank's investor, the Bank earns a fee. Let's call it 1% for ease of calculation.

$4,000 yearly interest payment x 0.01 = $40.

PC interest peeling fee: $40 per year per $100,000.

Estimate GSE MBS deal size = $1 Billion which translates into 10,000 $100,000 units. Multiply $40 x 10,000 = $400,000 profit per year on ONE full GSE MBS Securitization

Calculating profits on $5 trillion in GSE MBS securitizations

As referenced, the GSEs claimed to have securitized some $5 trillion in underlying first mortgages over the years beginning 2000 through the mortgage meltdown in 2008. One trillion dollars equals 1,000 billion dollars. Most calculators don't go that high. So for the fun of it, if we take the $5 trillion and do the math, here's what we get:

- Loan amount markup: $1 billion x 5,000 = **$5 trillion (one time**, up-front cash from investors)
- Loan Interest stripping markup: $40 million x 5,000 = **$200 billion per year**
- PC interest peeling fee: $400 million x 5,000 = **$2 trillion per year**

The Federal Reserve is used to dealing in these kinds of numbers.

Answering the question of why the Fed keeps dumping hundreds of billions into the GSEs.

For those who have been scratching their head and wondering why in the world the Federal Reserve keeps sinking hundreds of billions of U.S. Taxpayer dollars into two losing enterprises like Fannie Mae and Freddie Mac, the answer is simple. Trillions of dollars in cash flow in to the Feds coffers and those of its member banks.

Windfall to Member Banks since the financial crisis of 2008.

Prior to the financial crisis of 2008 the majority of America's financial assets were controlled by many hundreds of banks. After the reorganization it is controlled by a handful of banks.

The Fed manages America's economy in an economy of scale.

The sheer size of new money interest in the GSE securitization market place is the proponent that out runs the quantity of underlying single mortgages on single properties. This is the same scenario we've gone over in Private Label Securitization only with a different twist. The Commodities aspect (Chapter 2) and the Ponzi aspect (Chapter 4) still apply. Only this time the U.S. Government did not pull the plug as they did with the Private Label Securitizations (Chapter 5).

Instead, led by the Fed, the U.S. Government continues to promote the scheme by continuing to provide U.S. Taxpayer funds that allow the GSEs to continue paying the interest on the $1x to $4x GSE MBS Securitization sales to investors.

Same problem. Only $1x underlying mortgage. The MBS derivative price of $4x is determined by supply and demand, the $1x underlying commodity. The difference here is that the U.S. Government has gotten rid of the competition (Private Label Securitizers) and is now doing it themselves, using the GSEs. These two GSEs can evaporate in a moment, they are corporations whose stock is already near valueless. All the money we calculated for fun, the numbers too big for regular pocket calculators, goes to the U.S. Government augmenting U.S. Taxpayer dollars. The GSEs are a money maker.

The Federal Housing Administration ("FHA") a division of the Housing and Urban Development Authority ("HUD") on the other hand, is a potential U.S. Taxpayer bailout facing deep trouble. Unlike the GSEs Fannie Mae and Freddie Mac, the U.S. Government insures the underlying loans of FHA.

Chapter 12

FHA insured loans, the Next Bailout

Candidate

We've learned why the Fed bailed out and continues to bail out
Fannie Mae and Freddie Mac GSE MBS Securitization with hundreds
of billions of U.S. Taxpayer dollars.

The Federal Housing Administration ("FHA") began insuring loans for
small fees in 1934. The FHA is part of the U.S. Housing and Urban
Development ("HUD").

Since the financial crisis of 2008, more pressure has been put on The
Federal Housing Administration ("FHA"). Enough so that the FHA may
be the next bailout candidate.

FHA doesn't securitize loans. FHA however is integral to Government National Mortgage Association ("Ginnie Mae" or "GNMA") MBS Securitization, which we will come to learn more about in the next chapter (13). In this chapter we will address how the FHA stepped in when the mortgage market dried up as a result of the financial crisis of 2008 and now may be at risk of failing in a manner that could again require billions of dollars in U.S. Taxpayer bailouts.

The Federal Housing Administration (FHA) was created in 1934 by President Franklin D. Roosevelt to insure mortgage loans to borrowers who needed government assistance. Borrower's whose credit was often challenged in a transaction that was often very highly leveraged, meaning little cash down payment and lots of mortgage.

As a result of the Mortgage Meltdown of 2008 new purchase and refinance loans through regular mortgage banking channels dried up nearly overnight. Mortgages were just not being originated. This fueled the downward spiral of real estate prices.

The basic problem has been revealed in the regular annual FHA reporting to Congress and by authorities reporting on the issue.

Sensible loan limits existed prior to 2008.

Before 2008 under the National Housing Act FHA mortgage loan limits allowed borrowers in need to obtain a mortgage up to about 95% of the average house prices in the thousands of counties across America that FHA insures loans. FHA had lower limits based upon percentages of the GSE conforming loan limits at that time. For example, FHA would limit the loan amount to 87%.

FHA loan limits up to 125% of the average market value of a house.

As a result of the Economic Stimulus Act ("ESA") enacted in February 2008, FHA limits on mortgages originated after 03/01/2008 in qualifying programs could go to 125% of the average market value of a home. Limits were set to generously more (for example 175%) than the GSE Fannie Mae and Freddie Mac mortgage limits. In certain areas such as Hawaii and Alaska that limit was 150% of average market value.

FHA has violated it most important capital reserve regulations.

FHA's insurance reserves for losses against defaulting loan loss has violated its most important capital reserve regulations. Without sufficient reserves against expected and unexpected future losses, FHA can require hundreds of billions of dollars in capital infusion. Money that would have to come from U.S. Taxpayers, or in the case of America's huge deficits, by borrowings from those creditors of America already lending America money. Foreign countries for example.

As a result of the financial crisis, borrowers couldn't get mortgages. The FHA stepped in and covered upside down situations. Meaning made loans that were more than the market value of the property to borrowers whose demonstrated credit promised large defaults. Post 2008 FHA traveled the same path as GSEs Fannie Mae and Freddie Mac, overextending itself dramatically.

Bad and getting worse as the number of unemployed Americans increases. In 2012 about 23 million Americans were unemployed. Currently now at the publishing of this book in Fall 2016 the U.S. Bureau or Labor Statistics is reporting 94.6 million Americans are Not-In-Labor-Force. This is a staggering 29% of the entire U.S.A.'s population.

FHA is in critical condition. Added to the 94 million currently unemployed we must factor in house values that have declined from pre 2008 levels on homes that continue to experience negative equity in the property (loan amounts more than property values). As a result, the FHA continues to have less money in their insurance fund to cover. With the outlook bleak on record deficits and unemployment looking forward, FHA is in critical condition.

Originally FHA was required to have about 2% of reserves to fund losses. At the end of 2010 the FHA reported insuring somewhat under $1 trillion in loans ($870 billion) and the reserves were about ½ of one percent instead of 2%. This isn't to say the FHA is broke. They reported at that time having a little more than $30 billion in total reserves. Clearly, the FHA is operating as a high risk entity now. This potential teetering on the fence is another part of the potential crisis America is facing at the time of this writing.

When traditional lenders aren't making loans and the FHA is the major game in town the result is FHA going from insuring somewhere around 6% of all loans made in 2007 to somewhere just under 1/3 of all new homes purchased as of the 2010 report.

As of this writing, FHA now insures over $1 trillion in loans. Prior to the Mortgage Meltdown 2008 hopeful borrowers speculated before the real estate bubble burst in 2008. FHA is essentially hoping that robust real estate prices will solve the problem. By 2012 FHA had already paid out over $35 billion in only the prior few years to cover defaults. Current numbers for those interested, can be gleaned from their annual reports to Congress. We don't need to follow the exact numbers, we only need to understand the problem which continues to grow with the demise of private label securitization.

If we are going to rely on credit ratings agencies for guidance, as we did in the pre Mortgage Meltdown 2008 MBS Securitization debacle, we should not fully rest our hope in Moody's Analytics and S&P home price indexes to support FHA predictions. The adage might be "been there, done that and still paying the price for that error in judgment".

Anyone can go online and review the actuarial statistics. They are hoping home prices increase so cover mortgages that are more than the market value but if home prices decline or move sideways the FHA is going to require U.S. Taxpayer bailouts in the form of help from the U.S. Treasury.

In 2012 the Obama budget submitted to Congress provided the FHA with the first bailout FHA has required since it was created in the Great Depression. Luckily, the National Association of Attorney General's historic mortgage settlement made in February 2012 included about $25 billion paid in by the five biggest loan servicers in America. Ally/GMAC, Citi, Wells Fargo, Bank of America and JPMorgan

Chase. So the budget projection changed because FHA was slated to get some $1 billion of that settlement.

FHA weighs considerations to increase its premiums and up-front fees charged. According to FHA executive testimony before Senate subcommittees hearing the issue, the FHA is scrambling and doing a juggling act. Some may recall the $787 billion economic stimulus package the Obama administration offered which included $8,000 tax credits to first time homebuyers in an effort to prop up housing markets. FHA reported it lost at least $10 billion on 2009 and 2010 loan originations insured, in that little fiasco.

FHA has similar programs to the failed programs of the GSE and Private Label MBS Securitizations. These involve indemnification agreements with loan originators to cover FHA losses when loans defaulted, or were discovered to have other defects such as missing loan ownership documentation, loan fraud and/or poor underwriting.

The reality is, of those agreements represent a miniscule amount, somewhere in the 1/10th of one percent range of loans originated. In other words, somewhere in the neighborhood of 1,000 agreements on a little under 1 billion loans insured. Less than a drop in a bucket.

Nitty Gritty of MBS © 2016 Richard M. Kahn

In February 2012, Bank of America and Citigroup got caught certifying mortgage loans for FHA insurance that didn't qualify. Penalty: Bank of America agreed to pay $1 billion and Citigroup about $158 million. FHA's average number of loans insured was just under 1 billion loans. Another prop-up infusion of money to FHA.

Having the U.S. Government in the game today, gambling on home prices, after watching mortgage meltdown 2008 occur on the same premise is cause for grave concern.

FHA loans are financed with Ginnie Mae MBS Securitization.

Chapter 13

Ginnie Mae Government MBS Securitization[8]

In this chapter those with FHA, VA and other Ginnie Mae guaranteed loan types can learn about their securitizations.

When a Ginnie Mae loan foreclosures it is very rare to find any MBS Securitization toxicity involved. Homeowners with Ginnie Mae loans facing foreclosure are often misled into thinking they have traditional MBS Securitization defenses and can waste good money hiring

---

[8] Some information may have been gathered and confirmed from the government program's web site or publications.

attorneys, auditors and others who will happily take their money only to find in the end that they cannot thwart the foreclosure.

The Government National Mortgage Association (Ginnie Mae or GNMA) Mortgage Backed Securities (MBS) programs guarantee securities that are backed by mortgage pools. The securities are issued by lenders called "Issuers" and require approval by Ginnie Mae.

Ginnie Mae is the primary financing facilitator for all government Federal Housing Administration (FHA) insured and U.S. Department of Veterans Affairs (VA) guaranteed loans. Both of which are backed by the full faith and credit of the U.S. Government as to payment of principal and interest.

There are other loans that Ginnie Mae guarantees: The U.S. Department of Housing and Urban Development (HUD), the U.S. Department of Agriculture (USDA), the Office of Public and Indian Housing (PIH) and the Rural Development Housing (RD) and their select programs.

Unlike Fannie Mae and Freddie Mac, Ginnie Mae is not the actual investor, it doesn't buy the loans itself. It insures the mortgage pool bond certificate holders for a fee.

Two of the basic residential Ginnie Mae programs are the Ginnie Mae 1 MBS and the Ginnie Mae II MBS.

In the Ginnie Mae I programs all the mortgages bear the same interest rate and are formed by a single issuer. Multi-family loans can be in the pools. The issuer can make separate payments for each pool directly to the investor who owns Ginnie Mae certificated securities of that pool.

In Ginnie Mae II programs interest rates can be fixed or adjustable and vary. Only single family mortgages can be pooled. The pooled loans can be formed by single issuers or multiple issuers. Issuers and servicers make payments to a central paying and transfer agent (CPTA) who makes a single consolidated pass-through payment to each MBS security holder each month. The issuer and/or their servicer is responsible to make the mortgage payments collected to GNMA.

The best place to find information about all the programs and services GNMA offers is on their official web site: www.ginnemae.gov.

The Ginnie Mae securities are known as pass-through certificates, meaning they pass the interest and principal payments received on mortgages in the pool, through to the investor owners of the GNMA securities. This avoids double taxation (corporate then personal). Any pass-through amounts include deduction of a guaranty fee paid to GNMA and servicing fees paid to loan servicers of the underlying mortgages. In this way they operate in the classic Government Sponsored Enterprise (GSE) fashion.

GNMA has implemented a level of its own insurance into the transaction before they are required to pay holders on defaulted loans in the pools. This is where GNMA moves off into its own realm of GSE. When borrowers fail to make payments or miss payments for any reason, the Issuer can use any insured or guaranty payments (such as FHA or VA) to fund shortfalls and if those do not cover the full amount Ginnie Mae makes up the difference. In exchange for this guarantee, Ginnie Mae charges a fee. That fee is stipulated in the REMIC prospectuses and for example, may be 0.6% (0.006) of the principal amount each year.

Fannie Mae and Freddie Mac issue their own corporate guarantees to make payments whereas Ginnie Mae is backed by the full faith and credit of the United States.

The issuer is responsible for servicing all the loans in the pool and administering the securities to investors. Subcontract servicers are permitted on some functions, but not all. They must be a Ginnie Mae approved issuer and meet all the requirements for maintaining Ginnie Mae issuer status.

Issuers are responsible to acquire the mortgages, form the pools, perform servicing and obtain an eligible document custodian. There can be only one document custodian for the entire MBS pool. Strict document safekeeping standards must be followed. Issuers have the responsibility of marketing the securities issued.

Any mistakes made by the loan servicer in terms of errors that cause missed payments or underpayments must be borne by the servicer. For example, short falls in insurance or escrows for taxes and failure to adjust mortgage interest rates on time.

Mortgages that are found to be defective or that default are allowed to be substituted within a given period, in similar fashion to typical MBS REMIC standards. If the loan defect is not cured or replaced within a specified time, going forward through the MBS pool's life, the Issuer has to repurchase the mortgage loan out of the pool or loan package at the full face amount received by the issuer at the time the loan was sold to Ginnie Mae. That amount is referred to as "par".

Par is adjustable by any principal amounts advanced by the Issuer. This is typical to MBS standards. Atypical is the clout Ginnie Mae maintains to insure compliance over its issuers. An issuer who does not immediately buy a defective loan back when Ginnie Mae requests, knows that Ginnie Mae can call ALL their loans in default as a result, and the issuer may have to buy all the loans they have issued in the past back. Similar in fashion to Fannie Mae and Freddie Mac, Ginnie Mae provides a loan desk to accomplish these tasks.

Ginnie Mae's shining star performance in forcing defective loan repurchases stands in stark contrast by comparison to the failures of Fannie Mae and Freddie Mac to force defective loan repurchases by their issuers. That failure of Fannie Mae and Freddie Mac has become a financial burden born by U.S. Taxpayers as the Federal Reserve

Nitty Gritty of MBS © 2016 Richard M. Kahn

dumped hundreds of billions of taxpayer dollars into both Fannie Mae and Freddie Mac's publically traded corporations; and continues to do so.

Ginnie Mae's guaranty appears on each certificate purchased.

GUARANTY:

The undersigned, pursuant to Section 306(g) of the National Housing Act, hereby guarantees to the registered holder thereof the timely payment of principal and interest set forth in the above instrument, subject only to the terms and conditions thereof. The full faith and credit of the United States is pledged to the payment of all amounts which may be required to be paid under this guaranty.

GOVERNMENT NATIONAL MORTGAGE ASSOCIATION

By:_____

In Ginnie Mae transactions the Document Custodian reviews the loan documents of each Issuer for each pool and each loan package and certifies that they accurately represent the bundle of pooled mortgages. The Document Custodian then holds and safeguards these documents for the life of the MBS pool.

Nitty Gritty of MBS © 2016 Richard M. Kahn

Ginnie Mae MBS are initially issued in book entry form into the Central Registry (Register). Investors may request actual certificates to be issued and registered to themselves or a designee. The Register includes pool number, certificate number, name, address, EIN for each security holder, the original principal amount of the security, date of issue, interest rate, initial payment date and maturity.

Ginnie Mae provides a loan lookup tool for Issuers. Ginnie Mae does not report loan level information to the public[9]. *"The Ginnie Mae Loan Lookup enables mortgage borrowers to quickly determine if Ginnie Mae Lend America/ Lending Key owns their loan by providing a Loan Number and a ZIP code."*

There is a disclaimer on accuracy of data. *"The data contained herein was originally provided to Ginnie Mae by Ginnie Mae Issuers. Ginnie Mae makes no warranty, express or implied, on the accuracy, adequacy, completeness, legality or reliability of the data. Ginnie Mae hereby disclaims any liability associated with use of this data or any damages resulting from third party use of this data. This disclaimer applies to both isolated and aggregate uses of information."*

_____

[9] https://www.ginniemae.gov/lendamerica/searchLA.asp?Section=Issuers

Nitty Gritty of MBS © 2016 Richard M. Kahn

The Issuer is responsible for all aspects of the transaction and reporting is included. Issuers have access to the Document Custodian and forms to request holder in due course original loan level documents such as the Note and Mortgage.

Nitty Gritty of MBS © 2016 Richard M. Kahn

Chapter 14

SPE Bank Securitization

The following terms are all different accepted names of the same bankruptcy remote MBS bank to bank, off balance sheet Securitizations. A Special Purpose Entity ("SPE") can also be called Qualified Special Purpose Entity ("QSPE") or Special Purpose Vehicle ("SPV"). We can use them interchangeably.

Private Label MBS Securitization and bank to bank mortgage bank loan originators and aggregators utilized SPE-QSPE-SPV-Bank to bank MBS securitization in trillions of dollars of MBS Securitization.

SPE Bank Securitization issues are a common aspect of certain wrongful foreclosure cases where the MBS Trusts are not identified. One of the key symptoms is a loan that was originated by a particular lender who failed and now a different lender is trying to foreclose. There may be endorsements on the Note, or an endorsement in BLANK, or a trail of endorsements in blank that are being claimed authentic and the basis of rights and authority by a party seeking to foreclose.

> ➢ Investigations by the Author, a seasoned expert, finds many of these claims are contradicted by undisputable facts due to their nature and sources.
>
> ➢ Findings and information such as this by a party such as this can be presented in court for consideration as evidence by a Judge or Jury.

Special Purpose Entity (SPE) mortgage securitization is very "secretive", a term you may recall was used in the Ponzi chapter (4) by the SEC as a "red flag".

SPE securitization is regularly performed by banks and financial institutions interested in removing the mortgage liability from their balance sheets, creating cash and extinguishing risk of default on the loans. Banks and thrift institutions sell mortgages in this manner to maintain acceptable capital ratios required by the regulatory agencies.

Nitty Gritty of MBS © 2016 Richard M. Kahn

Mortgage banking institutions that originate loans themselves or buy loans from other lenders and mortgage brokers utilize SPE securitization as a regular part of their ongoing businesses. They have a mortgage lending and acquisition program. They cache the loans in their Loans to Sell portfolios. These financials are available in the corporation's annual report filings submitted to the SEC in publically traded MBS securitizations and required public company annual report filings.

In the Private Label Securitization chapter (7) the topic and methods of Special Purpose Entity (SPE) were identified. The SPE (called SPV) in that situation takes loans, then converts them into Certificate securities with the assistance of a CDO Manager.

A brief summary of key points presented in the Private Label Securitization chapter 7: In between Sale 2 Sponsor to Depositor and Sale 3 Depositor to MBS Trust, the SPE facilitated mortgage loans in, certificates out. The certificates were sold to the MBS Trust of investors for cash or cash equivalent (wired funds for example).

Prior to January 1, 2010, the SPE model was used and could qualify under accounting guidance related to mortgage servicing right (MSR) assets and liabilities; and be represented as a Qualifying Special

Purpose Entity (QSPE). As such, assets and liabilities were not required to be consolidated for financial reporting purposes. This made the transactions "invisible" on interim consolidated income statements and annual reports.

Effective January 1, 2010 new accounting rules eliminated the QSPE designation. Now the entities were required to be analyzed as to whether they constituted a Viable Interest Entity (VIE). If the bank believed they did, the SPE had to be consolidated for financial reporting purposes.

The Financial Accounting Standards Board ("FASB") issued FIN 46R. "FIN" stands for FASB Interpretation Number. The R stands for Revised. The FASB publishes Generally Accepted Accounting Principles ("GAAP") that U.S. Corporations can use in their accounting and reporting.

If the mortgage bank that sold the mortgage loans to the SPE retained a controlling interest that was not based on the majority of voting rights, it was determined that they were the primary beneficiary and needed to consolidate and report the assets and liabilities. Thereby making them visible on accounting reports.

FASB FIN 46R became elaborated in FASB ASC 810-10. "ASC" stands for Accounting Standards Codification and represents a major change in how GAAP authoritative literature is organized. FASB ASC broke down the thousands of non-government accounting pronouncements and reassembled them into some 90 or so topics to simplify their use and understanding.

It is important in analyzing bank securitizations to understand consolidated income statements and reporting. The complex corporate ownership structure finds different entities controlling financial interests.

In addition to cash from sale of mortgage loans in the securitization process, other assets were received. These included retained interests such as the Mortgage Servicing Rights (MSRs) and residual interests in the form of retained certificate ownership. These activities often represented significant earnings which were passed on to shareholders of the SPE.

Being able to hide these assets and liabilities and not have to report them created invisibility by use of the QSPE model. The SPE model was designed to provide transparency.

Nitty Gritty of MBS © 2016 Richard M. Kahn

When the SPE is a VIE (Viable Interest Entity), reporting the assets and liabilities on the consolidated accounting statements is required. The entities participating in the creation and use are left to interpret their participation.

The consolidated accounting becomes an important source in the process of determining if a loan was securitized in the invisible SPE, QSPE, SPV or the visible VIE or bank to bank method.

Certain actions or attributes of a SPE which does not need to consolidate its assets and liabilities on consolidated for financial reporting purposes and is therefore invisible, can turn into a VIE that has to consolidate assets and liabilities and report which makes them visible. If the SPE was thinly capitalized so that there was insufficient equity at risk to support the SPE's activities or the group that held equity did not hold substantive voting rights and could not control the entity, or the economics of the transactions didn't coincide with the voting interest (the anti-abuse rule); it was a VIE and had to have its assets and liabilities consolidated and reported.

The SEC has its own rules, regulations and guidance, as does the Internal Revenue Service (IRS). The FASB ASCs (Accounting Standards Codification that represents a major change in how GAAP authoritative literature is organized) do not change the GAAP (Generally Accepted Accounting Principles) or SEC requirements of accounting for public corporations. Their purpose is to make a very complicated set of guidance easier to research and use. Many U.S. Taxpayers feel a simplification of personal taxation guidance is very much desired.

Discovering QSPE securitization involves reverse theorem logic. Sometimes in foreclosure we find a lender is sticking to their guns that they continuously owned a loan originated between the years 2000 and 2008 as a portfolio loan. Making the case otherwise includes a process that utilizes "reverse theorem" logic. Stated simply to mean figuring out what something is not or does not have the attributes of, and you wind up clearly concluding what it is.

Once clue of SPE sales for example, is when the party claiming to still own the loan is found on its books to have sold $115 billion of this type of loan in the years since loan origination. Continuing the reverse theorem logic in a securitization investigation will be based on clues that roll on from there. Unless the particular loan number can be found in an MBS Trust somewhere, this will be a SPE ownership investigation and there are numerous ways to verify or challenge ownership.

SPE MBS Securitization is designed to be secretive, vague and ambiguous. This relates back to the Evaluating Ponzi Characteristics Chapter 4.

➢ To a seasoned securitization expert there are numerous ways to make and substantiate cases like this. They often involve interim party purchaser and seller investigations as well. Sometimes one can search one issuer's loans securitized shortly after the loan was originated and discover the loan on a list of loans identified for purchase.

➢ Enhancements to investigations into MBS Securitization Trust ownership often include side investigations into the SPE parties and interim participants.

Chapter 15

Farmer Mac MBS Securitization[10]

The last form of MBS Securitization to present is Farmer Mac MBS Securitization. If you are interested or are involved with farm, ranch or agricultural property and mortgages, this is the Government Sponsored Enterprise (GSE) that has done much to help farmers in America, which in turn has helped other Nations who depend on American agriculture and ranching. President Ronald Reagan's Administration implemented Farmer Mac.

The manner in which these Farmer Mac MBS Securitized loans are made and issued does not produce significant toxicity which

---

[10] Some information may have been gathered, confirmed or quoted from the Farmer Mac GSE web site farmermac.com or other government publications.

undermines the rights and authority of those seeking to foreclose. Farmer Mac loans are rarely able to be challenged on that basis. For this reason they are mostly outside the loop of typical securitization investigators examining mortgage foreclosure fraud. But they are securitized and their history and application is interesting. A party claiming to be a securitization expert will also exhibit knowledge of Farmer Mac MBS Securitization.

Here is a brief look at the essentials.

In 1987 a bill called the Agricultural Credit Act of 1987 (the "1987 ACA") provided credit assistance to farmers, strengthened the Farm Credit System ("FCS") and amended the Farm Credit Act ("FCA") of 1971. The 1987 ACA established a federally chartered Federal Agricultural Mortgage Corporation (FAMC) more commonly known as Farmer Mac.

The 1987 ACA was introduced in July of 1987, passed the House in October, passed the Senate in December and was signed by President Ronald Reagan on January 6, 1988; which enacted the bill.

The 1987 ACA made some important changes to the Farm Credit System (FCS). It provided assistance to distressed institutions, minimum capitalization requirements for FCS institutions and restructured the FCS with mandatory mergers of Federal Land and intermediate credit banks. These mergers resulted in the Farm Credit Banks.

The 1987 ACA established guidelines for State farm loan mediation programs and matching grants. Amendments allowed borrowers to use the same collateral to secure two or more Farmers Home Administration Loans ("FmHA").

The 1987 ACA created the Agricultural Mortgage Secondary Markets. This meant uniform underwriting, appraisal of the underlying security, repayment standards, mortgage pools, guarantees for qualified loan pool interest and principal payments and standards for marketing.

Farmer Mac was established as a GSE corporation whose stock traded publically. The corporation issued obligations to cover its guarantee losses. Farmer Mac began to follow Fannie Mae and Freddie Mac in the agricultural property niche. The secondary marketplace for Farm and Rural loans was born. Liquidity was provided to lenders. Foreclosure rights to redeem properties were enacted. Lenders could form pools of loans as issuers and in so doing could make loans and get them off their books right away.

Farmer Mac benefits lenders, borrowers and investors, as well as farmer, ranchers and those who rely on them.

Important segments of rural America benefit from Farmer Mac programs. Segments include farmers and agricultural businesses as well as ranchers. Community businesses are also serviced and include schools, fire and police stations (first responders). Co-ops, more properly called Cooperatives, which also benefit include utilities and other entities such as cooperatives that also act as borrowers.

Lenders also benefit
Lenders that service the segments above can include institutions in the Farm Credit System, credit unions and insurance companies as well as commercial banks or mortgage companies working in the segments.

Farmer Mac conducts its activities with three basic programs.
Farmer Mac I, II and Rural Utilities. Farmer Mac II LLC is a subsidiary of Farmer Mac.

Nitty Gritty of MBS © 2016 Richard M. Kahn

Farmer Mac 1 provides three product options to finance farm and ranch first mortgage loans through the secondary investor marketplace.

Farmer Mac purchases the "guaranteed" portions of loans which are guaranteed by the U.S. Dept. of Agriculture (USDA) in varying programs.

Farmer Mac has a program in which the ICBA (Independent Community Bankers of America) who are approved as Farmer Mac I sellers, stand to receive valuable benefits from Farmer Mac's secondary market in this program.

Farmer Mac also provides loan documentation services through a preferred document preparation provider for Farmer Mac known as PPDocs, Inc. Farmer Mac lenders and sellers can prepare their own documents or use PPDocs.

Appraising

Farmer Mac appraisal valuation is beyond the scope of most general residential property appraisers. Loans sold to Farmer Mac and serve as the security to the promissory notes may have unique qualifiers. A core requirement is identifying the value for loan to value calculations to understand the property market value and risks. Appraising these types of properties and the security they provide to the borrower's financial strength for income and producing properties enables Farmer Mac to understand the borrower's capacity to service the debt over the long term.

Rural, agricultural, farm, ranches and making loans to cooperatives that supply them are not what we could consider "vanilla" appraisal jobs. In many instances the comparables and market prices are complex.

Farmer Mac and the American Bankers Association (ABA)
Farmer Mac also has an alliance with the American Bankers Association (ABA) through Business Solutions, a subsidiary of ABA. In this manner ABA member banks can receive important Farmer Mac I benefits such as preferred pricing, rates, products and a streamlined approval process for becoming a Farmer Mac approved Seller.

Farmer Mac offers their Portfolio Program.
Bank lenders in general, need to get loans off their books to manage their capital ratios, maintain liquidity and succeed in the lending business. The capital ratios must be maintained to regulated levels.

Farmer Mac issues what are known as LTSPCs, Long Term Standby Purchase Commitments. In exchange for annual fees, Farmer Mac can agree to a future purchase of loans from acceptable mortgage pools. This enables lenders to retain mortgages in their portfolio but reduce their risk and exposure on portfolio loans from 100% down to 20%. Lenders can portfolio loans until they are paid off, refinanced, or become delinquent.

Farmer Mac also issues AgVantage, a program which allows lenders and institutions to borrow money by pledging qualifying loans owned in their portfolio as security. Once approved the lender can issue AgVantage securities backed by Farmer Mac guarantees, sell them to investors and thereby raise more capital to lend.

Investors who purchase Farmer Mac securitizations can do so in different ways. Buy Agricultural MBS (AMBS), buy common stock (equity), or buy unsecured senior debt (bonds) in the capital markets.

Farmer Mac has three classes of common stock which can purchased on the New York Stock Exchange under the ticker symbol AGM.

- The regular class C of non-voting common stock can be owned by anyone. The non-voting aspect is unusual because most common stock comes with voting rights.

- The class B stock is voting stock but may only be held by Farm Credit System institutions.
- The class A can only be held by institutions that are not part of the Farm Credit System. These would included banks and other financial institutions, with a limit of not being allowed to own more than 1/3 of the outstanding common shares of class A stock.

Farmer Mac is specialized and modern (GSE)

The aspects of Farmer Mac offerings and features mentioned above reveal a specialized and modern Government Sponsored Enterprise (GSE) that offers a high standard of information, learning tools and dedicated support for participants.

If you own a Farmer Mac loan and want information, contact your loan Servicer.

Farmer Mac offers detailed program information online.

www.farmermac.com provides a wealth of information and resources online.

Chapter 16

MERS – Tool of Deception

Identifying misrepresentations, defects, deception and foreclosure fraud in MERS assignments and affidavits by MERS employees or robo-signers, is a basic defense in litigated foreclosure. MERS actions and issues are often misinterpreted and misconstrued. One reason is, it's not actually MERS, it's employees of loan servicers seeking to foreclose that are directing the foreclosure and representing MERS.

The group of operations we refer to simply as MERS.

MERSCORP Holdings, Inc. ("MERSCORP") was founded in 1995. It is a privately held Delaware corporation based in Reston, Virginia. MERCORP's subsidiary, the Mortgage Electronic Registration Systems, Inc. ("MERS") serves as the original mortgagee of record on tens of millions of mortgages recorded in county property records.

MERSCORP owns and operates the MERS® System, which is the database registry where loans registered to MERS are recorded. MERS began operating in 1997. MERS maintains a website at www.mersinc.org

The principal owners that founded MERSCORP include Fannie Mae, Freddie Mac, The Mortgage Bankers Association ("MBS") who represents all segments of the real estate finance industry both residential and commercial, Bank of America, CitiMortgage, GMAC, HSBC, JPMorgan Chase, Wells Fargo and the American Land Title Association. Many of the bank members are or were Federal Reserve member banks.

Warning, if an owner won't eat at their restaurant maybe we shouldn't either? Some of the original members such as Bank of America, JPMorgan Chase and Wells Fargo did not utilize MERS on their loan originations. Presumably as founding members they clearly understood the potential failure of improperly recorded chain of title. These members still record mortgages in the traditional manner at the local county property recorder's offices where the property is located.

Nitty Gritty of MBS © 2016 Richard M. Kahn

MERS boasts 5,000 or so members.

It is estimated that some 3,000 were banks prior to the financial crisis in 2008. The rest were mostly lenders and mortgage servicers.

MERS charges fees to their members.

- Annual membership fees range in size depending on the size of the member. From about $265 up to $7,500.
- Whenever MERS is the mortgagee of record on a loan, MERS is paid a $6.95 fee by the member.

MERS was mortgagee of record on over 65 million loans.

65 million was the number of loans from MERS' inception until the mortgage meltdown in 2008. By 2010 that number dropped to about 33 million loans outstanding. Loan volume was reduced via sale, refinance , satisfaction and unfortunately for most, massive amounts of foreclosures as a result of mortgage meltdown 2008. MERS has been a key pivotal component in 10's of millions of foreclosures.

MERS employees have numbered from 5 to around 50.

Pretty astonishing for a company that is involved as Nominee for the Lender on 10's of millions of loans. MERS endows lender and servicer employees to represent themselves as MERS executives. In the earlier years it was rumored MERS only had around 5 employees.

Giving the Wolf keys to the Hen House

MERS has effectively done away with the age old system of transferring mortgage ownership, recording the chains of ownership on mortgages in the property clerk's office of the particular county where the property is located.

MERS private database system purports to act as a legitimate public tracking entity. Loan servicer employees are taking actions as MERS executives.

- In foreclosure this translates to empowering the hungry wolves to care for the tender chickens, at their sole discretion.

This sealed the fate of myriad homeowners facing foreclosure. Lenders and loan servicers portraying themselves as MERS did not have the proper traditional evidence of chain of title ownership. So they reverse engineered claims and documentation to foreclose. These loans were not properly sold, transferred, recorded, executed or assigned properly. Under traditional lending premise, this would find a lender losing a foreclosure case.

MERS does not provide title insurance in a traditional manner.

In traditional title insurance recordation of ownership, the title company does a title search of prior owners and registers the transfer of title ownership at a closing with the property recorder's office. They collateralize their actions with Title Insurance, paid by a premium. In this manner, if a mistake was made, the Title Insurer would pay for losses incurred. While MERS promised many benefits to Investors and Lenders, title insurance was not one of them. So those victims of questionable title transactions were and are confronted by absorbing their own losses in case of errors or omissions by MERS or MERS employees. This was a critical disservice by MERS and affects the 10's of millions of mortgages MERS is on.

MERS Rules and Policies empowered Servicers to game the system.
Servicers step in and take title and transfer recordation actions well after the time of closings. MERS employees regularly doctor the loan ownership documentation, fabricate endorsements, assignments and transfers. Parties seeking to foreclose such as lenders and servicers, use and direct their own employees and agents to take ownership actions and sign as MERS executives.

Robo-signing and forged signatures by the thousands per day.
MERS ownership and transfer documents are regularly found with forged signatures of purported MERS employees. MERS and Servicer

affidavits by employees representing they have personal knowledge, do and did not. Researching facts for affidavits takes time and robo-signing hundreds a day did not offer time to research when you do the math to see how long it takes to just sign that amount of documents a day in conveyor belt operations.

It is well documented in Court case transcripts and deposition testimony over the years since 2008 that the purported "affiants" had no idea what they were signing. They had no knowledge of the information behind the information contained within that they claimed to have personal knowledge of. The didn't even fill in the information within the affidavits other than signing on the line. In a predominant number they didn't even sign, it was a signature stamp. In a many cases they admitted to not even placing he stamp. Nevertheless other employees acted as notaries and swore that the affiant was before them personally signing, when that was distinctly untrue. The same was also true for co-signers and witnesses.

MERS has been the target of Federal Agency investigations which resulted in Consent Orders against it for the aforementioned lack of oversight. MERS was found fostering these unsafe unsound foreclosure practices in the aftermath of mortgage meltdown 2008.

At the root of the problem was MERS and MERSCORP's failure to oversee servicing and foreclosure actions involving MERS.

MERS sold the idea of its registry as a boon to county property recorder's offices. MERS touted, counties would save money because there would be less mortgages to record which translate into less employees needed and less hours needed to work. In reality, property recorders no longer received their recording fees on some 65 million mortgages each time the mortgage transferred. Typical MBS Securitization involved 3-4 interim true sales on each underlying mortgage. If we include SPE bank securitizations (detailed in Chapter 14) that number increases.

MERS claimed it could assist regulatory law enforcement in detecting mortgage fraud. MERS touted it could track social security numbers, names and property addresses. Instead, as MBS Securitization investor demand was so high, underwriting standards of loans were lax and rife with both lender and borrower fraud. Borrowers were obtaining loans with no evidence of income, no evidence of assets, not only with no money down but in many instances taking cash out from the loan transaction. Loans were early defaulting in record numbers. We find little or no occurrences of this claimed detection being recorded on the record by MERS.

Nitty Gritty of MBS © 2016 Richard M. Kahn

MERS represented a major benefit was enabling county records to know who was servicing loans. MERS claimed the ability to advise county records offices who the owners were that held the Notes. MERS presented this as important, even though Notes were never and still are not required to be recorded in county property records. In reality the county property clerk's tax records included the owner. Tax bills went to the owner or the registered Servicer as the case might be depending on how escrows were allocated to be paid.

MERS claimed to be the central recipient for receipt of mail as the mortgagee. Another representation purported by MER to be important. But MERS itself only had 50 or less employees. MERS relied on loan servicers to receive mail. In reality county property recorder's knew how to get hold of the owner or the servicer to notice and collect taxes, they'd been doing it for hundreds of years.

MERS systems bypass recordation on chains of mortgage ownership in county property records. The act of MERS recording transfers of ownership in their own proprietary database system, has resulted 65 million mortgage loans bypassing traditional mortgage registration in local property clerk's offices. In addition to the problems of unregulated Servicer employees taking actions on chain of title, which undermines the legitimacy of transfers, no fees were paid to the property clerks. County coffers across all U.S. States have suffered billions of dollars in losses of revenue.

MERS claimed to solve the logistical nightmare county recording offices would face, recording millions Assignments. This turns out to be another falsity by MERS. Doing the math undermines their claim.

Assume it takes ten minutes to intake, scan and file the paperwork.
- 1 million loans at 10 minutes each for recording requires 46,296 hours. (1,000,000 / 10minutes = 10mm minutes / x 6 = 46,296 hours).
- Divide 46,296 hours by a 40 hour work = 11,575 work weeks.
- Divide 11,575 work weeks by 50 in a year. Equals 231 workers working one year to process the 1 mm loan transfers.

America has 3,144 counties, including county equivalents
As of 2013 it was reported that America has 3,144 counties including county equivalents.
- With 3,144 county recording offices, assuming only one per county, 231 working full time over a year would mean only one employee in every 136 county recording offices could record 1 million mortgage transfers.

- Extrapolating out, the 66 million original loan transfers done over 7 years (2000-2007) equal 9,428,571 per year.
- Each loan was transferred about 3 times on average in the chain of ownership to MBS Securitization Trust. So the 9,428,571 loans per year x 3 transfers equals 28,285,714 loan recordings required per year.
- Above we calculated 231 annual county clerk employees could process 1 million loan recordings per year. To perform 28,285,714 transfers per year would require 6,533 employees.
- Divide the 6,533 employees required by the 3,144 county recorder's offices in America translates into about two full time employees (actually 2.07), with a little overtime thrown in.

The monetary cost to County Recorder's Offices.
- Let's assume the annual salary of a recording employee is $50,000 with benefits.
- 6,500 employees x $50,000 per year is $325 million per year.

County recorder fees for processing mortgage recordings
- Let's assume $30 per recording, a number offered by MERS in 2010 around the time its CEO gave testimony before Congress.

Nitty Gritty of MBS © 2016 Richard M. Kahn

- We have 66 million transactions x 3 parties in the average chain of title. This is 198 million transactions.
- 198 million transactions x $30 each equals $5.94 billion dollars.
- Divided by 7 years equals $848.5 million per year.

Gross profits to County Recorder's offices

Based on the above calculations it would take 2 employees in each of the County Recorder's offices across the USA to process mortgage transactions at a cost annually of $325million. The fees on only 3 transactions in the chain at $30 per recording is $848.6 million. The profit on that is $523 million (over 1/2 billion dollars). Or about $166,348 profit per year to each county recorder's office.

The calculations above do not include sales after the purchase of MBS securitizations.

MERS charges about $7 for each transfer to their Members.

In the example above, if you take the 66 million individual transactions multiplied by a 3 chain of sale for 200 million individual recordings, MERS earned nearly $7 each (actually $6.95). That is nearly $1,4 Billion dollars earned by MERS.

In the final analysis, MERS took away nearly $6 billion from our counties and earned nearly $1.4 Billion in the process.

Somewhere, somehow, our government politicians and regulators swallowed the MERS lies of efficiency and money saving aspects to Counties, hook line and sinker. Looks like our politicians did not do the math and did not hire an expert to do it for them.

Let's examine how MERS operates in a mortgage transaction.

MERS summarized their role simply:

According to MERS[11], they have *"over 3,000 members who have registered more than 65 millions loans on the MERS® system since it began operation in 1997"*. MERS claims to provide the mortgage industry with three important services.

- *"Tracking information about mortgage loans on the MERS® System, a database that tracks changes in a loan's servicing rights and ownership.*

- *MERS acts as a common agent (or "nominee") for the mortgage finance industry and can serve as the nominal mortgagee of record on behalf of its member for loans*

---

[11] Taken from MERS Quick Facts Brochure made available to the public on the MERS website www.mersinc.org

registered on the system. Every MERS mortgage agreement contains paragraphs that explicitly designate MERS as the mortgagee and give MERS the authority to act on behalf of the owner of the loan.

- *As the mortgagee of record, MERS receives legal notices and other mail regarding the mortgaged properties, which MERS sorts, scans and transmits electronically to the appropriate party for each loan, based on information in the MERS® System."*

MERS appears on a Mortgage/Deed of Trust

The typical mortgage/ deed of trust that includes MERS will state (usually towards the bottom of the first page) that *"MERS is a separate corporation that is acting solely as nominee for Lender and Lender's successors and assigns. MERS is the beneficiary under the Security Instrument. MERS is organized and existing under the laws of Delaware, and has an address and telephone number of P.O. Box 2026, Flint, MI (48501-2026) tel. (888) 679-MERS."*

Looking further into the typical mortgage with MERS (often on page three just above the Borrower Covenants section), it will clarify: *MERS as nominee for Lender and Lender's successors and assigns, has the right: to exercise any and all of those interests, including, but not limited to, the right to foreclose and sell the Property; and to take any action required of Lender including, but not limited to, releasing and cancelling this security instrument.*

MERS as Nominee is the key to the process and defenses

MERS didn't hand Lenders and Servicers a carte blanche to do what they wanted as they wanted when they wanted. That wouldn't be ethical and it wouldn't pass muster. MERS rules require MERS officers to act as Nominees on written instructions from the Lender, successor or assign that owns the loan. It is a proxy system. The owner gives the MERS officer the right to do this or that. Not the right to transfer ownership away from the owner and continue to do what a MERS officer pleases.

Federal Consent Orders against MERS identify unsafe and unsound foreclosure practices directly caused by lack of supervision by MERS of lenders and servicers employees acting as MERS executives.

MERS has and continues to be at the epicenter of wrongful foreclosure. Servicers and parties seeking to foreclose regularly record documents in county property records and submit documents drawn by MERS (loan servicer employees) into court that are the basis of wrongful foreclosure claims. The MERS problem is epidemic.

What MERS is found and fond of doing is acting as if they have received proper written instruction from a real holder in due course owner when in fact that is not the case. They fabricate, falsify and misrepresent, which makes it unlawful even though they aren't being prosecuted (yet) for that.

MERS purports to act as nominee for the holder in due course owner but in many cases, this just isn't possible. For example, MERS is

- representing to act as nominee for a lender who has closed its doors and is defunct.
- purporting to act for the original lender and not the holder in due course owner.
- purporting to transfer the mortgage and the note, a note in which they have no ownership rights in to transfer.
- purporting to transfer loan ownership to MBS investors, conspicuously absent inclusion of intervening true sale owners in the chain of title ownership along the way.

When in fact MERS has no standing to foreclose or pass legal ownership of loans on to others. Some revealing facts about MERS and their assignments:

- MERS is never conferred any economic benefit.

Nitty Gritty of MBS © 2016 Richard M. Kahn

- MERS never collects money from borrowers, whether under the Note or Mortgage.

- MERS will not realize the value of any borrower's property sold through foreclosure, or in the event the Note is paid.

- MERS has no financial interest in the Note.

- MERS will suffer no injury if the Note is not paid.

- MERS will realize no benefit if the Mortgage is foreclosed.

- MERS does not satisfy requirements of constitutional standing (real party in interest), nor do they satisfy prudential standing (having a financial stake) in the property or loan.

- The MERS executive (as the MERS published rules denote) is an employee of the loan Servicer.

- MERS is not entitled to payment from the borrower.

- MERS does not enforce the security for non-payment.

- MERS never performs a single loan servicing function.

MERS facilitates the art of Reverse Engineering proper chains of title and ownership. MERS bypasses traditional recording at local property clerk's offices This enables MERS servicer employees to basically do as they wish or are instructed. There is no chain of recorded title on property recorder's records to contradict claims in MERS transactions.

MERS servicer employees seeking to foreclose but do not have the proper documentation to do so find MERS servicer employees attempting to reverse engineer the chain of title. Backdating documentation to make it appear legitimate in court when it has been fabricated after the fact. Robo-signing is a key component to reverse engineering as well.

Robo-Signing

Robo-signers are employees of the servicers or their document processing vendors. Robo-signers work together or separately but are brought together on documents to pull off this documentary misrepresentation years after the actual mortgage chain of ownership transaction took place. These employees are designated to represent and sign the documentation. Signing is their job. They get paid to sign. They have no idea what the details of the transactions they are actually signing. They are signing what the bosses put before them, usually in stacks. All day they sign and sign and sign. Then the Servicers record and submit these signed documents into foreclosure cases that the Servicer's attorneys litigate to foreclosure. We even see employees of the Servicer's attorneys litigating the case signing as third party executives in this ruse, it is not uncommon.

The typical example finds 3 robo-signer employees acting together.

Nitty Gritty of MBS © 2016 Richard M. Kahn

Employee 1 prepares an Assignment, filling in the names of the purported original or subsequent owners. is the corporate executive of a third party who claims beneficial rights and authority (the MERS executive). Employee 2 is a Notary. Employee 3 draws up the legal documents from templates and has little understanding of the content. Employee or affiliated employee 4 sends the documents to Employee 3 that are to be used. Employee 4 can be a foreclosure mill attorney for the Servicer or a document generation firm like Lender Processing Services ("LPS"). None of the employees have done a shred of research into what they're signing but they all need their jobs so they do what the boss tells them. Sign. The transfer takes seconds and there is a table with rubber stamps, set out for convenience.

MERS skeleton staff empowered Servicer's staff to wield the guillotine of wrongful foreclosure. In claiming to be holder of record or nominee, MERS is on tens of millions of loans. That represents a major number of mortgages in the United States. One would expect MERS to have a huge staff of employees. That is not the case. Instead as touched on above, MERS has empowered its "members", mostly mortgage banks and loan servicers, to designate their own employees to act as MERS "officers".

This has enabled loan servicers to basically assign mortgages to themselves and create transfers and assignments to whomever they wish in the process of seeking to foreclose and present legitimate ownership to a court when that just isn't true. It's contrived. The loan servicer is fostering or bringing a foreclose on a loan they have no money loaned out on and do not in reality know who the proper legal owner is.

This has resulted in millions of foreclosures conducted without obtaining the documentation to evidence proper chain of title, rights or ownership and authority normally required in a foreclosure.

We find many cases where legal ownership has not been established.
Authority has not been provided in writing by the note owner who can establish that ownership in the manner of proper chain of title. Proper litigation and expert investigation can expose bogus, contrived, falsified and fabricated claims of ownership when it truly does not exist.

MERS has been the cause of what we now find to be tens of millions of questionably conducted foreclosures that may have actually been done in an unlawful manner.

MERS participation passes "under the radar".
MERS continues to serve its purpose by the front seat passenger seat. In terms of trying to be in the driver's seat, they tried but failed at bringing foreclosure actions in court in their own name.

Much of the confusion resolves around the "nominee" issue.
The process under MERS rules[12] is that "the "note owner" NOTIFIES MERS that there is a default on the note and instructs MERS (in writing) *as the note owner's agent and the mortgagee,* to assign the mortgage lien to whomever the note owner chooses to be the foreclosing agent (typically the servicer for the mortgage loan). The assignment of the mortgage is recorded on the MERS System, not in the public county land records. MERS member employees can basically juggle this any way they want. The highly respected, highly trusted, tried and true honest reliable Chain of Title recording by county property records is no longer involved.

MERS confuses holder in due course ownership.
This is important to understand. The promissory note evidences ownership, not the mortgage. Notes are not recorded, they are

---

[12] *FINAL MERS and the Foreclosure Process 05-23-2011.docx3*

Nitty Gritty of MBS © 2016 Richard M. Kahn

endorsed, negotiated, delivered and accepted. Only the mortgage is recorded.

MBS Securitization is based on multiple true sales from origination to MBS Trust investors.

When a mortgage is originated and then sold, the initial owner was the owner but now an endorsement on the note makes the new owner the owner/holder in due course. If they have given the servicing to a third party then the holder in due course transfers the mortgage separately. Possession of the mortgage entitles servicing rights and authority to the servicer in possession. Should the servicer assign, transfer or sell their mortgage servicing rights, they transfer the mortgage via MERS to a new servicer. Each sale of the note is evidenced by an endorsement on the note and the last purchaser is the "current' holder in due course owner.

What many MERS employees foreclosing do is try to "wiggle" the Sale of the Note language into the MERS assignment. Alone the MERS assignment only transfers loan servicing rights. Together with the Note it transfers legal ownership. As we've learned above, MERS is NEVER the legal owner of the Note. MERS Rules stipulate that language "selling" or "together with the Note" is non-compliant. But once the hungry wolves are set on killing the chicken, there's not much to stop them. Especially considering tens of millions of foreclosures and a MERS only maintaining a handful of skeleton staff at MERS itself. More empty promises from MERSCORP.

Assignments are made by MERS to the loan servicer or designated party and that party will bring the foreclosure action.

Loan servicers provide the day to day administration of loans with the borrowers.

In the case of non-payment the loan defaults and servicers are required when necessary to file foreclosure. The mortgage backed securities (MBS) trusts who acquired the mortgages were required to have the properly conveyed ownership documentation. The reality is, in very many cases, it appears they did not obtain this documentation. Discovery of widespread false and misleading claims by MERS to have beneficial ownership interest in foreclosure cases has prompted MERS to *forbid* their members to file foreclosure in MERS name anymore.

MERS provides public access[13] to discover who the current loan servicer is.

---

[13] https://www.mers-servicerid.org/sis/

Nitty Gritty of MBS © 2016 Richard M. Kahn

With your borrower's social security number you can also find out who the supposed investor owner is.

One big problem with this process is the fact Servicer employees acting in their MERS capacity as designated MERS officer, has access to the system, controls the input and makes the reporting. This allows conflict of interest and errors or misrepresentations to occur. In essence the system is self serving to the members, the banks and loan servicers. MERS allows low level employees of servicing lenders to control data entry on the MERS website. Allowing loan servicer employers to instruct employees on data to enter provides the opportunity to manipulate the records. These employees are far from the third party lofty entitled executives whose positions they portray when they sign.

MERS Rules and other information may be found with Internet access.

MERS has tightened access on their web site since the foreclosure crisis. Passwords and member logins may be required, depending on the information sought. A lot of MERS documentation has been downloaded from their web site and posted on the Internet.

Some routine aspects of MERS operations may require Discovery requests made in Court.

Nitty Gritty of MBS © 2016 Richard M. Kahn

The MERS MIN (Mortgage Identification Number) is readily accessible on the loan documents.

An eighteen digit number that allows you at access the loan servicer and investor for a particular loan, based upon what the MERS Certifying Officer (loan servicer employee) is instructed to enter into their database. In this manner lenders and loan servicers control the MERS data. MINs are on mortgages, deeds of trust, and may have a reference on a Note. They may also be on Riders to the Mortgage.

The MERS MIN Summary

Can be generated by any member or certifying officer and contains a summary of the transaction history recorded on MERS. This includes the address of the property, whether it is an active or inactive registration, whether MERS is On the Mortgage (MOM), the lien position (first, second, etc.), the date registered, county, primary servicer, borrower, co-borrower if any, pool number, note amount, custodian, investor, interim funder, originating organization, property preservation company, batch number, transfer type, status, transfers and sales; dates of occurrences and more.

The MERS Milestone report

Nitty Gritty of MBS © 2016 Richard M. Kahn

Obtained for a particular MIN number loan. Contains headings of description, date, initiating organization/ user and the milestone information. That information can include the MIN status (active or inactive), new servicer, old servicer, new owner, old owner, interim owners, batch number, sale date, transfer date, particulars of each and more.

MERS MIN Summaries and Milestone reports

Easy as pressing a button to obtain for those with access. Difficult for the borrower side to obtain without discovery or court order in a foreclosure case. The reason being, an experts reviewing the entries can often discover material defects and discrepancies in the foreclosure claims that undermine rights and authority to foreclose.

MERS members routinely mislead courts and borrowers in deceitful ways.

One of those ways was to foreclose in MERS own name, as if the Worker was actually an owner of the mortgage (using our Repo Man scenario). This blatant lie was so egregious and conspicuously false that it became the focus of several state attorney generals. In 2011 with a change in the rules MERS began to act before the actual foreclosure and do their transferring to the loan servicer and facilitating the foreclosure in that manner.

Many feel and argue that it **is a fraud upon the court to fabricate and falsify an assignment** just prior to the foreclosure taking place or at any other time.

But for the millions more homeowners facing wrongful foreclosure now, there is hope. Homeowners and their attorneys are becoming more knowledgeable. So are Judges.

Mortgage loans in MBS Securitization process can become paid off and that's the reason the MBS investor owners aren't balking when Servicer's employee MERS actions seek to win real estate by wrongful foreclosure which goes into the Servicer's Real Estate Owned portfolios and not to the MBS investor.

Chapter 17

Credit Enhancement, Bailouts and Insurances

Credit enhancements were at the root of Credit Ratings Agencies (for example: S&P ,Moody's and Fitch) raised the marginal underlying borrower's credit up the highest investment grade AAA. As a result investors were willing to accept much less interest than the borrower's loan interest payments. In an ideal world of course. In reality the credit enhancements were not sufficient to cover the rampant defaults when mortgage meltdown 2008 hit.

Yet credit enhancements were the promises upon which premise was based. In reality, many mortgage defaults were paid off with credit enhancements. the high numbers of defaults were just too much to cover all the way.

Let's take a look at some reasons a MBS Securitization Trust investor's underlying mortgage loan securing their Certificate of ownership may have been paid off and ownership of an actual underlying mortgage loan is floating around and up for grabs.

When a loan is paid off and floating in the ether so to speak, the Servicer knows. The Borrower and Investor do not. This knowledge enables a party seeking to acquire the mortgage without ever lending the money or paying the rightful owner for the mortgage, to do so by falsifying ownership documentation in the process of bringing a wrongful foreclosure and not getting caught. Even when they do get caught, they only lose the right to foreclose and the legal fees they paid. They don't go to jail.

Credit Enhancement lessens risk to investors and increases profits to Securitizers. In MBS securitization, credit enhancement is a form of financial support against loans in the pools defaulting. Credit enhancement drastically increases profits to the securitizers. High investment grade credit ratings such as AAA mean investors are willing to accept lower interest return, and the securitizers can strip off profits.

Here is an example that doubles the yearly cash flow and one time sale profit. Take an 8% interest rate on an underlying mortgage loan. Use $100,000 principal amount for ease of calculation. That's $8,000 a year cash flow from borrower mortgage payments. If the credit ratings of that cash flow were materially increased, say by Credit Enhancement, up to Investment Grade such as AAA as many MBS Securitizations were, MBS investors may be willing to accept 4% or $4,000 for their $100,000 investment. That leaves $4,000 free cash flow and an extra $100,000 additional profit to sell elsewhere to other MBS Trust investors. More detail in the Interest Strips Chapter 18.

Credit Rating Agencies determine the rating of MBS Securitization Trust certificate groups. Credit Ratings Agencies ("Ratings Agencies") include such companies as Moody's, Standard & Poor's and Fitch. There are others. These are the top 3 in the industry.

Ratings Agencies evaluate MBS Securitization Trust assets and rate them. Their ratings are intended to help investors determine the likelihood that the returns and obligations the issuers offer in their prospectuses and offering memorandums will be met.

A more favorable rating means investors would accept a lower rate of return in exchange for the financial security of their principal invested. Lower ratings mean having to pay more interest to attract the investment dollars.

Generally speaking, at the top of the Ratings you have the most secure investments. At the bottom of the ratings you have Junk Bonds, which are highly speculative and risky investments. Institutional investors requiring safe sound investments put their money in the top tiers of the credit ratings, BBB to AAA for example. Having top tier credit ratings means the investment bankers could attract the massive investment dollars these types of foreign and domestic institutions have at their disposal to invest.

Credit ratings agencies are not credit reporting agencies.
Credit reporting agencies include TransUnion, Equifax and Experian. These companies rate individual's personal credit.

Ratings Agencies are supposed to be objective when they investigate the Issuers.

Issuers seeking a Credit Rating will pay fees to a Ratings Agency to provide this. The Ratings Agency analysts dig into whatever financial aspects of the underlying obligations and issuers the analysts are interested in obtaining. The issuer provides all documentation and details the analysts ask for.

Credit Enhancements were overvalued by Ratings Agencies.
This was at the root of the problem causing the mortgage meltdown 2008 and collapse of financial markets. Ratings agencies had earned decades of trust. Ratings Agencies systemically overvalued the risk reducing qualities and strength of credit enhancements in MBS Securitizations.

Underlying credit ratings of borrowers in the mortgage pools was miscalculated. Borrower's individual credit scores at the time of their applying for and receiving mortgage loans were noted on each underlying mortgage in the MBS Securitization process. What was not factored in properly by the Ratings Agencies were the individual terms of the mortgages themselves and the likelihood of default due to monthly payments that would or could drastically increase.

Underwriting Standards in Private Label MBS eroded as investor demand for MBS increased. Investment banks had so many investor outlets for raising capital in MBS Securitizations that commercial banks and mortgage banks had to lower their standards of borrower credit and alter the terms of mortgages to make mortgage origination more attractive and generate more loans. In doing so, borrowers took out loan whose terms were attractive initially but degraded dramatically as payments adjusted.

The willingness of borrowers to accept a lower interest rate over a short term such as 1-2-3-5-7 years that would adjust to a higher rate was in large part influenced by the real estate market during the boom years preceding the mortgage meltdown 2008. Real estate values trended upwards between 2000 and the collapse in 2008, in large part fueled by available mortgage money in the marketplace.

Borrowers were no longer long term investors for equity and cash flow. Trading in real estate for near term profits fueled price rises and satisfied MBS Securitization needs with more purchase and refinance mortgage originations. It was not uncommon for borrowers to leverage rising equity in properties to refinance, take cash out and invest in other properties. Many homeowners that were not real estate speculators were jumping on the band wagon.

When real estate prices went down, instigated by the mortgage meltdown 2008 and financial crisis, underlying mortgages began to default in massive quantities.

Credit enhancements were designed to support the demonstrated default statistics looking back. These were projected to be a very small percent. Sometimes as little as 1%. As defaults spiraled out of control and large percentages of entire portfolios began to default, credit enhancements could no longer provide financial support. In hindsight, Rating Agency analysts did not predict the massive loan defaults. It all flows back to the secrecy and complexity involved, that was covered in the Evaluating Ponzi Characteristics of the Mortgage Crisis, Chapter 4. Even the Ratings Agencies were fooled. They shouldn't have been, experts with this knowledge were and are out there.

Excess spreads

When mortgage loan interest payments exceed the interest paid to investors and Issuers retained a portion of it, the unsold portion could be earmarked as excess interest to use and offset any defaulted loans in the portfolio to specific classes of Certificates.

In other words, using our example above, if there was $8,000 in interest coming in and investors were only receiving $4,000, the extra $4,000 excess spread could be used to enhance assurances that the initial $4,000 cash flow promised was well covered.

As we will learn in the next chapter on Interest Stripping (Chapter 18), MBS Securitizing issuers would sell varying amounts of these excess interest payments to other investors. The amount they did not sell could be retained as excess spread for Credit Enhancement.

Over-Collateralization

When MBS Securitization issuers contributed more face value of mortgage loans than the investor's investment in the MBS Trust, this is over-collateralization. Theoretically this lowered the risk of defaults on the mortgage portfolio purchased by the individual MBS Securitized Trust.

In reality the over-collateralized mortgage loans were often loans of such low borrower credit rating that the securitizers could not get their credit ratings up to investment grade so the promoters held these loans as equity. And in many cases it was these extra loans that served as the over-collateralization promise. A worthless promise in many cases because of their high risk and high rate of default once the loans adjusted.

In hindsight, the massive defaults of underlying loans in the pools far outstripped the value of any over-collateralization once the cushion of performing loans in the pool could no longer support the defaulted payment loss.

Subordination

This method allocates losses first to lower rated holders, such as the Junior debt Certificates in a process of securing higher rated holders, such as senior debt Certificate holders. In the case of losses, the junior debt absorbs them first. Losses would be absorbed by the most junior bond certificate note holders and work its way up the ladder to the most senior debt holders.

In other words, the classes of senior debt were paid first. Funds could be allocated from lower rated debt holders to pay senior debt holders in a form of robbing Peter (the lower rated investor Certificate holders) to pay Paul (the higher rated investor Certificate holders).

In MBS Securitization Trusts where subordination exists, there is a substantial conflict of interest potential that results in Trustees and

Servicers representing them deny loan modifications to otherwise deserving borrowers. If a loan mod that benefited senior certificateholders harmed junior certificateholders, this was a conflict of interest that could result in class action lawsuits.

For example: a borrower's loan was in Group A. The holders of group A loans are senior certificateholders. The junior certificateholders are subordinating their interest payments, and suffer a loss if the payments on senior certificateholders are not met. The loan defaults and faces a loan mod that could lower payments. Lower payment would mean a locked in loss each month payable by the junior certificateholders to make up the shortfall. The junior certificateholders will object to the senior certificateholders allowing a modification of their loan.

The reverse would occur for instance, if a loan held in Group B owned by the junior certificateholders faced default and a lower payment loan modification. If the loan were modified, the subordinated security interest pledged by the junior certificateholders to the senior certificateholders would be supported by less income. That would be unacceptable to the senior certificateholders.

For this and other reasons, REMIC provisions limit the amount of loan modifications permitted in MBS Trusts. These rules were relaxed in the wake of the financial crisis and will be addressed in the REMIC Chapter 20.

Insurance Guarantees against default of underlying mortgages can protect specific classes of MBS Certificates, in specified amounts. It is not uncommon for MBS Securitized Trusts to include the purchase of outside third party insurance to cover losses or defaults in specified groups of Certificate. Typically, the groups that would benefit are the Senior most secure groups. Fees for the insurance are paid to the Insurer. A policy is issued. The terms of the policy are defined. The terms and specifications are presented to both the investors via the offering memorandums and prospectuses, and the credit Ratings Agencies.

Massive losses to certain monolithic Insurers such as AIG and Ambac as a result of the mortgage meltdown 2008, caused insurers to face bankruptcy. The ripple effect this would have on corporations, government and economies who relied upon these companies in offering their own separate investments to raise capital would be devastating. For example, bond offerings with insurance guarantees to raise their credit ratings so the interest rates they paid were lower, required those insurances to stay in place. For this reason, these insurers were too big to fail and as such were recipients of T.A.R.P. bailouts as a result of the financial crisis.

Homeowner's insurance does not insure revenue to the MBS Securitized Trust investors. The insurance guarantees protecting MBS investors is distinctly not Homeowner's Insurance that is taken out when the loan is originated and maintained on the loans. This insurance only protects the Lender, their successors and assigns (subsequent owners of the loan) and the borrower. Homeowner's insurance covers damages to the improved property (not the land) and liability of claims made by people who may become injured on the property.

Credit Default Swaps

Commonly known by their initials, "CDS" or simply "Swaps". MBS Trusts may arrange to pay fees to third parties for insurance that protects the investors against default of underlying mortgage assets. The arrangement typically involves an initial payment and then multiple payments over time. The MBS Trust buyer is the insured and the Insurer is the seller of the policy. In exchange for the premiums paid by the MBS Buyer, the seller insures the specified Certificate class against defaulting loan losses. The CDS swap terms specify an amount up to which the Seller agrees to be financially liable. For example, a $1 billion MBS might find the top $250 million tier provided with a CDS against underlying mortgage default for any reason up to and including $250 million in aggregate losses. This type of CDS in place influences Credit Ratings Agency ratings given to the class(es) of Certificates covered by the policy(s).

Creation of the Credit Default Swap (CDS) to insure against underlying mortgage defaults is generally credited in the industry to JPMorgan Chase, one of the founders of MERS. CDS were structured ahead of MERS rolling out in the mid 1990s. CDS played a large role in MBS Private Label Securitization.

Credit Default Swap (CDS) to insure against underlying mortgage defaults should not be confused with the CDS issued against the estimated $1.5 billion dollars of Bond offerings by GSEs Fannie Mae and Freddie Mac that raised funds for their operations. The GSEs failure and placement into Conservatorship in 2008 triggered a credit event and those CDS settled on that issue, paying out in 2008.

Nitty Gritty of MBS © 2016 Richard M. Kahn

Chapter 18

Interest Strips – Profits in excess cash flow

Stripping interest from cash flow in the origination phase of MBS Securitization can produce substantial additional profits to the sponsors of MBS Securitization. The parties turned individual loans into profit making commodities they could sell and resell. In other words, the borrower's loans became the asset which the participants marked up and sold for profit over time. Initial sales occurred as early as at or near the time of loan origination.

Example of Interest Stripping: Take an 8% interest rate on an underlying loan. Use $100,000 principal amount for ease of calculation. That's $8,000 a year cash flow, paid by the borrower(s).

After enhancing the credit (fully described in last chapter (17) up to investment grade, which is BBB to AAA or the equivalent depending on the format of individual ratings agencies. If MBS investors were willing to accept 4% interest payment annually due to the high ratings, that would require payment to investors of $4,000 on each $100,000 of investment. That leaves $4,000 free cash flow or another $100,000 additional principal amount that could be sold to other investors. The vehicle of same could be derivative contracts or sales to other MBS Trusts of investors.

This initial interest stripping in MBS Securitization typically occurs between sale 2 and sale 3 in the private label securitization, as illustrated in Private Label Securitization Chapter 7. This is the "mortgages in certificates out" SPV operation conducted by the CDO Manager. Loans come in at X percentage and Certificates go out at Y percentage. Y always being less than X.

The multiple sales of underlying mortgages in MBS Securitization can occur very close in time to the MBS Securitization being issued. Typically days or weeks. This means that the borrower's loans are quickly turned into trading vehicles on the way to turning the $1x of borrower's loan into the $8x of total trades based on that loan in the marketplace. An example we have established herein early on.

Here is another example of a lower spread interest strip.

Investors may be receiving 5% on a loan that is paying 7.5%. In this case the borrower pays $7,500 a year on $100,000 loan amount. The investors receive $5,000. The difference is $2,500 and divided by 5% the markup is $50,000. On a $400,000 original loan amount that is $200,000 additional near term profit received by the Securitizers.

Net Interest Margin (NIM) Trusts

MBS Securitizations where the underlying asset is not a pool of specific singularly dedicated mortgages on real estate properties, and instead is an asset representing the excess interest on mortgages sold to other MBS Securitized Trusts are called Net Interest Margin (NIM) Trusts.

In Traditional Lending banks calculate their net interest margin profits (NIMs) on mortgages held in the similar manner. The difference in the spreads, minus expenses and allocations of respective defaults in the underlying portfolio, are profits reported on the bank's consolidated financial statements.

Traditional lending cash flow spread NIMs profits are exaggeratedly less than MBS Securitized NIMs profits. Traditional lending NIMs only reflect the difference in interest rate differential. The MBS NIMs reflect additional capital raised, upon which the NIM MBS pays the resultant interest.

For example: A Traditional lender's NIMs reporting on the balance sheet will show the interest spread as profit. If the borrower's payment is 8% on per $100,000 of loan amount and the cost to the bank to of the money to lend out is 4% then the profit is $4,000 each year on that loan.

On the MBS Securitized NIM, they are selling the 4% to an investor willing to pay $100,000 for it. This profit of $100,000 is received up front and the investor receives the 4% annual interest cash flow of $4,000.

A bank can do a lot more with $100,000 paid up front, than they can do with $4,000 that will trickle in over 12 months of payments. Especially when leverage and margin are applied. Definitions and Illustrations of Margin and Leverage are in Chapter 5.

NIM trust "corridors" of cash flows can and often are made into a complex class of securitized finance derivatives. Complex in terms of who gets what and when.

The NIM Notes can also be entitled to benefits of underlying Swap and Cap Agreements made by the insurer (a bank for example). Structurally, the underlying NIM cash flow should ideally come from a class of certificates in the pool that have not been sold before, to prevent further dilution of the underlying asset ($1x mortgage) securing the investment. In reality that is hardly the case and the NIM derivatives were reduced in the $1x to $8x model found to have occurred.

ARMs can be the subject of interest rate cap agreements.
Many underlying mortgages were fixed Adjustable Rate Mortgages ("Fixed ARMS"). Interest was fixed for a period certain before it became a regularly adjusting mortgage. For example 1-2-3-5-7-10 year fixed then adjustable.

The fixed rate is given. The adjustable rate is linked to a readily available index, such as the U.S. Treasury index. Readily available refers to where it is published. For example the Wall Street Journal or the Federal Reserve web site where Treasury Rates are published.

The adjustable rate is a combination of stated Margin that is added to the index. The margin that is added is set by the originating lender. The actual Margin rate is determined by the loan officer, mortgage broker or lender at the time of loan of loan application and locks in at loan origination. The Par Plus factor plays into the equation. Par Plus was defined in Chapter 8. The more the margin, the higher commission fee was paid to the lender/broker/loan officer at time of loan origination. Together the Margin plus Index equal the interest rate that a borrower pays on the mortgage Note in between adjustments.

Interest Rate Cap Agreements

Referencing the ARM section immediately above, in the interim payment stage in between interest adjustments, changes in the interest rates in the marketplace can be hedged using Interest Rate Cap Agreements.

Another example can occur when a borrower wants to keep the interest rate of a loan below the potential change of an underlying index rise that could cause a raise in their interest rates.

In an MBS Trust, the issuer may want to insure a steady predictable payment to the investors and enter into Interest Rate Cap Agreements to do so.

Some litigators use interest stripping as the basis to disgorge profits.

Chapter 19

Mortgage Servicing Rights - MSRs

Mortgage Servicing Rights are the contractual agreement between a legal owner and an agent of the owner who performs specific loan servicing functions.

In foreclosure we often find a loan Servicer claiming to be beneficial owner and holder with the right to foreclose.

> ➤ This is often misrepresented in a wrongful foreclose to imply that the servicer is the legal owner, meaning purchased the loan themselves or originated it and have the amount of the loan laid out of pocket when that is not the case.

Beneficial ownership is an equitable right given by a legal owner to take actions on the legal owner's behalf.

Nitty Gritty of MBS © 2016 Richard M. Kahn

Legal owner is the one who paid money for the loan and has the right, title and interest evidenced by an original Note with an endorsement to them specifically or an endorsement in BLANK and they hold the "paper", the original Note evidencing that.

Legal ownership vs. Beneficial Ownership

A Servicer's role is that of a paid agent of the legal owner, endowed with some beneficial ownership rights by the legal owner. These beneficial ownership right rights will be expressed in a written servicing agreement, wherein the legal owner authorizes the beneficial owner (loan Servicer) to take actions on behalf of the legal owner. Legal owners pay a stipulated fee to the loan Servicer for their day to day handling of the loan servicing responsibilities and endow these beneficial ownership rights on the loan Servicer.

Notes are not recorded

The original endorsed Note in the hands of the legal owner who paid for it does not get recorded in county property records. Nor does it get recorded with MERS (MERS is detailed in Chapter 16). It is in the possession of the legal owner or in the case of an MBS Securitization, the Note is in the possession of the Document Custodian.

Mortgages are recorded.

The original Mortgage that passes to the legal owner in the purchase transaction is recorded in the county property records. The recording will initially be in the name of the originator, the party who loaned the money to the borrower or in the name of MERS as Nominee for the Lender if MERS is on the Mortgage ("MOM"). (MERS is detailed in Chapter 16).

Mortgage Servicing Rights are often passed or assigned from one servicer to another. This passage of rights to act as Agent for the legal owner and service the mortgage are typically accompanied by an Assignment of Mortgage (AOM) recorded in the county property records or on a MERS loan, recorded in their MERS System. These AOMs which transfer servicing rights only will not stipulate "sell" or "together with the Note". They will stipulate "assigned" or "transferred".

The legal owner provides a copy of the Note to the loan servicer to evidence the legal owner's rights title and lawful ownership of the loan. In this manner owners demonstrate their lawful right to empower the loan Servicer as the owner's Agent, to act on the legal owner's behalf and service the loan. With a copy of the Note endorsed to the legal Owner and a proper assignment of the

Mortgage to the loan Servicer, the loan servicer then has beneficial ownership of the Mortgage and is "holder" of the Note. As holder in this manner, the Servicer is authorized by the lawful owner to conduct day to day servicing on the loan, interact with the borrower and if necessary foreclose on a defaulted loan.

- Often in wrongful foreclosure we find a loan servicer seeking to foreclose filing AOMs that improperly include "sell" and "together with the Note" when that power was not endowed under the Servicing Agreement. A power that is typically reserved by the legal Owner or their Trustee.

In MBS Securitizations the initial Servicer is called Master Servicer. In Private Label Securitizations this can be a servicing division of the originator or a servicing company hired by the MBS Trustee. In GSE Fannie Mae securitizations Fannie Mae is the Owner, Holder and Master Servicer.

Master Servicers rarely perform day to day loan servicing. Master Servicers are fully responsible for the loan's servicing but typically outsource these functions to what is called a "sub-servicer". The Master Servicer has the right to service but Servicing is a big job and requires specific functions that a Master Servicer maybe could perform but most often choose not to.

Nitty Gritty of MBS © 2016 Richard M. Kahn

Master Servicer takes a cut of the fees and passes the work on.

Lawful owners of loans allocate a gross percentage of the aggregate loan amounts as a fee allocated for servicing of the loan. This fee, in gross, is paid to the Master Servicer. The Master designates a sub-servicer and pays the sub-servicer a portion of the total gross loan servicing fee. The Master Servicer keeps the difference as gross profit between of what they receive from the investors and what they pay out for sub-servicing. Sub-servicers does all the work.

Sub-Servicers can pass on their responsibilities

It should be noted that sub-servicers, with the permission of the Master Servicer, can pass the work on to another sub-servicer in the same way, retaining a little of the spread from servicing fees or can simply bypass that and pass the entire responsibility on in succession to a new sub-servicer. One circumstance can be passing defaulted loan servicing on to a specific sub-sub-servicer (so to speak) who specializes in that activity.

Day to Day loan servicing functions are complex.

Servicers interact on a daily basis with the borrowers and interested parties to the individual loan. This can include:

- issuing welcome letters

- receiving and collecting monthly payments by various methods;
- answering demand requests
- answering borrower inquiries
- claims on property insurances
- notices of tax or insurance payment delinquencies on borrowers who pay these themselves and paying those payments if the servicer is paying those via escrow withholding from regular monthly borrower payments
- managing and reporting the monthly and annual escrow accounts
- issuing income tax statements to the borrower and lender or legal owner
- issuing payoff amounts
- evaluating and granting or denying payment deferrals
- reporting payment promptness or lateness to the Credit Agencies

When the monthly payments or payoff monies come in, the servicer typically deposits them the very next business day to the Master Servicer's trust account. The Master Servicer gets the use of this money in between the time it receive it and the time it distributes

Nitty Gritty of MBS © 2016 Richard M. Kahn

regular monthly payments to the legal owners of the loan or their Trustee in the case of MBS Securitized Trusts.

The sub-servicer is communicating and reporting to the Master Servicer, who is regularly reporting to the lawful owners of the loan on a regular basis.

The Master Servicer performs services and administrative functions in that capacity to the MBS Trust, in accordance with the pooling and servicing agreement. Basically, it does so in the same manner that it services and administers similar mortgage loans for its own portfolio. It takes into consideration the customary and usual standards of practice that mortgage lenders who act as servicers employ in the locale related to where the mortgaged properties in the portfolio of loans are physically located.

The Master Servicer keeps the overage as their share of sub-servicing fees paid. The Master Servicer deducts their mortgage servicing fee from the MBS Trust payments and pays the sub-servicer their agreed upon sub-servicing fee.

- **In a contested foreclosure**, It is recommended to request the Servicers produce copies of the Master and sub-servicing agreements to evidence authority.

Nitty Gritty of MBS © 2016 Richard M. Kahn

The Securities Administrator of the MBS Trust performs services to the Trusts according to the pooling and servicing agreements. The securities administrator is responsible for performing certain tasks and functions. They calculate the distributions of cash flow to the holder of Certificates, they make payment on the Certificates and they as a registrar and transfer agent for the MBS Trust

Lockbox Method

Payments between Master Servicers, Securities Administrators and Trustees of MBS Trusts may employ a "lock-box" or "lockbox" account. Commercial banks provide this service. They accept either electronic payments, wires or paper checks. Lockbox is quite efficient and has distinct benefits. The entire process is fully automated. No staffing required. There is a quick turn time clearing funds. A lockbox removes or reduces the chance of actual employees handling a transaction. Taking employees out of the mix reduces or eliminates chances of error, stealing, or otherwise defrauding investor funds.

Foreclosure

The Master Servicer and if appointed, their designated sub-servicer, are required to initiate, conduct and direct foreclosures against delinquent borrowers whose payments are in default for a specified period. Depending on their agreed upon policy on delinquencies and default, the servicer is required to begin reaching out in specified manner on delinquent loans. This means contacting the borrowers by mail, phone, even knocking on doors if necessary. Servicers can make certain modifications that allow a borrower in default to come back into current status. But loan mods are restricted by REMIC Rules (details in the REMIC Chapter 20) and the MBS Trustee's practical avoidance of a loan mod that would benefit one class of Certificates to the detriment of another (as detailed in the Credit Enhancement Chapter 17).

If the loans cannot be brought into current status and other sale or refinance takeouts of the loan cannot be accomplished, servicers are required to initiate and direct foreclosures in both judicial process (mortgages) and non-judicial process (deeds of trust) states.

Foreclosure Mills

Servicers typically align with specific law firms to accomplish the task of foreclosure on defaulted borrower mortgages. These law firms are sometimes referred to as "foreclosure mills" due to the high rates of foreclosures they can handle representing active loan servicers. In contested foreclosure litigation, attorneys representing either side are often referred to as "opposing counsel" by the opposite side.

Nitty Gritty of MBS © 2016 Richard M. Kahn

Mortgage Servicing Rights (MSRs)

The right to service a mortgage is an asset that accompanies a loan when it is originated. It can remain with the originating lender and be retained or it can be sold. These rights to service are called Mortgage Servicing Rights (MSRs).

Servicing Released Premiums (SRPs)

When lenders sell their loans with servicing rights, the lender will be paid more for the loan than if the lender retained their loan servicing rights. When this occurs that extra money is referred to as SRP or Servicing Released Premiums. SRPs are assets.

Outstanding loan amounts on Mortgages and Notes are liabilities.

A mortgage is carried as a liability on the books for the outstanding principal balance of the mortgage. Loans that held with the intent to sell are held in loans-held-for-sale, as a liability on the books. If and when the loan is sold, the liability is removed. Any income over and above the outstanding principal balance, plus any accrued expenses is profit that goes on the asset side of the balance sheet. Profits are assets once the transactions are completed.

MSRs are Assets

Lenders value their Mortgage Servicing Rights at fair value as an asset and may retain or transfer the servicing. As an alternative to transferring ownership of the MSRs, the owner may contract subservicing if allowed in the servicing agreement they have with the legal owner of the loan. If they transfer the servicing, they may still retain a portion of the total servicing fee. When this occurs the lender will appropriately value that reduced servicing fee portion at fair value as well.

MSRs represent a large multi-billion dollar industry.

It is not uncommon for large servicers to service millions of loans.

Let's examine the money side of loan servicing fees.

For our example we'll estimate the annual loan servicing fee is 1/3 of 1% or $333 per $100,000 of loan amount. On a monthly basis, this translates to just under $28 per month.

One MBS Securitization Trust may include $1 billion of loan amount. That represents $3.3 million a year in servicing revenue or $275,000 a month. For example: A $1 billion MBS Trust can own a mortgage pool of 4,000 loans at an average original principal balance at time of purchase of $250,000 each.

Let's figure out the residential MSR industry market.

The Board of Governors of the Federal Reserve System publishes the numbers of "Mortgage Debt Outstanding" in America at any particular time. This information is categorized in their Economic Research and Data reporting. This can be sourced online at www.FederalReserve.gov.

As of June 2016 the total outstanding Mortgage Debt in America from all holders (single family, 1-4 family, multi-family, non-farm non-residential and farm) is just under $14 trillion dollars. $13.848 to be exact. Farm is a small fractional percentage of this total. Curiously total outstanding has remained in the $13 trillion plus range each year across a look back reporting period since 2012, the date range on the current reporting. Breakdowns include:

- by property,
- by type of holder,
- GSE,
- FDIC,
- Mortgage Pools,
- Individuals and others.

Using the $13.848 Trillion total residential (and farm) mortgage debt in America, our prior calculation of 1/3 of 1% mortgage servicing fee represents $45.7 Billion dollars a year. Many loan servicers charge more. If we calculate the mortgage servicing fee at a 1% fee annually, the annual MSRs are nearly $150 billion per year.

Calculating the fair value of MSRs

This is a complex financial affair that is performed on a regular basis by loan servicers and reported on a regular basis. The calculations require present valuing estimates of future net servicing cash flows. The calculations take into consideration the actual and the expected. For example, actual prepayment rates, discount rates, servicing costs and other economic factors that are being experienced today. These can be compared with past experience and factored to estimate future factors. Using software provided by servicing platforms, systems can update in real time so that loan servicers and lenders know the value of their MSRs at all times.

MSRs are trading asset that changes hands

Loan servicers regularly sell MSRs to others in the secondary market place. These transactions are separate from the sale of lawful ownership of loans in the secondary marketplace. Loan servicers sell MSRs in the process of managing their balance sheets and financial capital, or to manage interest rate and loan default risks. Sales of MSRs in their own rights are often done in multi-billion revenue stream dollar packages and can represent many tens of thousands of loans.

Loan servicing transfers require recordation of some sort. Traditionally, this was done in the local property clerk's office with an Assignment of Mortgage or Deed of Trust. A fee was paid to the county clerk, the recording was performed and returned to the party making the request to record.

MERS has taken over this role. (Detailed in the MERS - Tool of Deception Chapter 16).

Chapter 20

REMIC Rules, avoiding corporate double taxation

Many of the actions in wrongful foreclosure, such as claims to transfer a defaulted loan to an MBS Trust or claims to transfer a loan after two years from the closing date or claims that an originator is transferring the loan to the Trust are easily undermined by the REMIC Rules. REMIC Rules prohibit these transactions.

Before we begin with REMICs, let's touch on REITS.
Borrowers whose original loans were purchased in a mortgage pool and sold to an MBS Trust may be facing foreclosure by a Real Estate Investment Trusts (REIT). This occurs when REITs have purchased defaulted loans and are either trying to foreclose for profit or are

offering loan modifications in an attempt to turn the defaulted loan into a performing loan and then sell the loan for profit once it is aged or seasoned as a performing loan.

Unlike REMICs REITs have pools of money from multiple investors and invest in multiple types of real estate projects including equity and mortgages. REITs are not static pools of assets like REMICs are. REITs act like real estate entrepreneurial businesses. They can actively buy, manage and sell a variety of asset groups.

REITs enjoy a similar tax pass-through like REMICs but the REIT operates as an ongoing business. A REIT therefore enjoys this pass-through by deducting dividends paid to its shareholders. It pays taxes on undistributed dividends, therefore REITS typically distribute all of their taxable income to their shareholders each year and as a consequence owe no corporate taxes.

REITs come in three different types or groups of ownership. All three types include selling shares of the REIT to investors.

- Equity REITs: Engage in various real estate activities for profit.
- Mortgage REIT: Engage in the purchase and sale of mortgage.
- Combination REIT: Engages in Equity REIT and Mortgage REIT activities.

REIT operations are complex, as are their tax rules.

For our purposes, REITs often invest in REMIC Certificates and buy mortgage loans from Default Loan Servicers that are non-performing. The intent on these non-performing loans is to either turn them into performing loans and sell them, foreclose on the properties and sell those for profit or modify the loan and hope it becomes performing at a later date.

REIT loan modifications

Those who wish to modify a loan owned by a REIT should understand the tax basis upon which REITs can modify. When a REIT takes a mortgage they own, let's say at a $100,000 principal amount and modifies it for less, let's say $70,000, the REIT must realize $30,000 in phantom income for tax purposes. That means profit they owe tax on without the actual profit dollars. It is strictly an accounting. If the REIT does not have qualifying losses to offset that phantom income, it is likely the REIT will not agree to this kind of loan modification.

REIT MSRs

REITs can invest in different kinds of real estate, including Mortgage Servicing Rights. REITs can also purchase loan servicers including default loan servicing operations.

REITs can also buy excess mortgage servicing rights eMSRs

MSRs were covered in the previous Chapter 19. Interest Strips were covered in Chapter 18. Excess Mortgage Servicing Rights ("eMSRs") occur when the originator or seller of loans in MBS Securitizations retains some portion of the MSR and/or interest in the underlying interest income (Interest Strip) on mortgage loans that have been securitized. REITs can purchase these eMSRs on the securitized mortgage loans.

These activities of REITs depend in large part on the interest rate environment. With low interest rates there is a significant business strategy in buying higher interest loans that have been securitized and try to turn them into profits in one of the ways discussed. They also depend on the real estate market. If REITs can foreclose on properties whose value is below the market, they can profit from that process as well.

REITs have different attributes than the MBS which is the subject of this book. Suffice it to know that REITs are and have the potential to continue to involve themselves with the underlying mortgages owned by MBS Trusts and the Servicing entities and MSRs.

Real Estate Mortgage Investment Conduits (REMICs) enjoy tax treatment benefits provided by Congress and regulated by the Internal Revenue Service. These REMIC Rules enable Mortgage Backed Securitization and govern the manner in which MBS operates. Much of the Pooling and Servicing Agreements, Prospectuses and other legal documents that create MBS encompass issues related to and cited the REMIC rules.

REMIC Rules are provided by an act(s) of Congress in 26 USC 860 Sections 860 A through G.

The U.S. Code is considered prima facie legal evidence of the law and statutes enacted by congress. Here are excerpts in pertinent part. Familiarity with the set of sections is encouraged for those contesting foreclosure where an MBS Securitization Trust is involved.

The IRS REMIC Rules Require certain actions and ***Prohibit*** deviation:

1. The only party to sells loans to the Trust is the party issuing Certificates to the MBS Trust (the Depositor).

2. MBS Trusts must buy performing loans. No defaulted loans are permitted to be purchased by the MBS Trust at any time.

3. All sales or substitutions of mortgage loans must occur within 2 years of the closing date, a/k/a the start-up date.

REMIC Rules avoid corporate "double taxation".

A corporation doing business for profit pays taxes in what is known as "double taxation". First the profits are taxed at the corporate rate and shareholders then pay taxes on the distribution of profits at their own personal rates.

The real estate tax sheltered aspect of REMCS provides a pass-through and shareholders only pay tax on a personal level.

The REMIC tax shelter benefits are a regulation created to prevent what were called highly leveraged real estate tax shelters where shareholders computed interest and depreciation in a certain way that enabled the shareholder to deduct over 100% of the capital contribution they made, from their taxes.

The 1986 Tax Reform Act did away with those highly leveraged tax sheltered real estate deals.

In its wake Congress enacted the REMIC Rules that identify acceptable deductions in the form of pass-through tax incentives. Congress enacted taxation of REMICs in Title 26 of the US Code. The Treasury regulations, better known as the Federal Tax Regulations are in 26 CFR (Code of Federal Regulations).

The REMIC rules govern Mortgage Backed Securities (MBS).

They govern the mortgages allowed, the business model allowed and provide timing restrictions and general rules. You can find these in the Internal Revenue Code (IRC) sections 860 A through G. At the end of this chapter the reader will find the 860A-G Code in pertinent part. The IRS has codified the USC 26 860 into its own IRS Tax Code, which is the IRS's right and obligation.

Draconian ramification for violation of REMIC Rules
If MBS violate REMIC tax code provisions, the IRS can enact draconian ramifications on shareholders and the MBS Trust. Adverse consequences include:

- 100% prohibited transactions tax on any gain realized from the deemed disposition and in some circumstances
- Imposition of a 100% prohibited transaction tax; and
- Failure of the entire REMIC to continue to qualify as a REMIC, thereby causing full double corporate taxation on all income derived from its mortgage assets pool.

There is a strict start-up date, called the "closing date" in MBS

In MBS declaring REMIC status, MBS Trust Agreements such as the Prospectus, Term Agreements or Pooling and Servicing Agreements in Private Label MBS, or the Trust Agreement in Government Sponsored

Enterprise (GSE) Fannie Mae, Freddie Mac, Ginnie Mae and Farmer Mac deals, define a Cut Off Date, a Closing Date and a 90 Days Date in compliance with IRS REMIC rules.

Only qualified mortgages can be purchased by a REMIC. MBS Trusts cannot purchase loans in default.

REMIC Rules require a strictly static pool of assets.

The IRS quotes Congress's intention in the Congressional legislative history. A REMIC "has no powers to vary the composition of its mortgage assets." [14] This "static pool aspect" of REMICs means the loans it purchases are the loans it owns. Unlike a REIT, a REMIC is not in the business of buying and selling loans as a business. It is in the business of buying loans and earning interest on the investment and liquidating the loans out of its portfolio.

- This also means that REMICs do not necessarily purchase loans from lists of loans offered up for sale to the REMIC MBS by aggregators or securitizers in the initial stages prior to the MBS start-up date a/k/a closing date. This is a common misrepresentation in wrongful foreclosures.

---

[14] IRC 860 in re: S. Rep. No. 99-313, 99th Cong., 2nd Sess. 791-92, 1986-3 (Vol. 3) C.B. 791-92

The REMIC is a Trust and has to have its powers vested in a Trustee. The Trustee is responsible for protecting and conserving the mortgage assets that represent the property of the REMIC Trust. The Trustee is not an associate in a joint enterprise with the certificate holders and is not conducting ongoing acquisitions of real estate and mortgage business for profit in the MBS Trust. Trustees have a fiduciary responsibility to conduct the affairs of the MBS Trust in their best interest.

Loan modifications are also under strict guidance. The IRS acknowledged the mortgage crisis and government loan modification efforts by Congress and provided extra leeway in the REMIC Rules to comply with certain efforts to prevent foreclosure. The Home Affordable Modification Program ("HAMP") is one example. The Home Affordable Refinance Program ("HARP") is another.

A critical component of qualifying as a REMIC is the acquisition of performing loans. Performing loans can best be described as loans which are not in default. Defaulted loans or non-performing loans cannot be transferred into the REMIC, at any time. It is strictly prohibited.

Potential transactions that my violate REMIC provisions must have an Opinion of Tax Counsel. Most if not all MBS Securitizations require an event of such potentially catastrophic results, such as selling a loan to a REMIC after prescribed dates or accepting a defaulted loan can only be made with a majority percentage of all investors agreeing in writing (usually 2/3^{rds}) and an Opinion of Tax Counsel that the acceptance of ownership after the REMIC closing and 90 day dates would *not* have adverse tax consequences. This will be filed with any Investor disclosures and kept on permanent record in the MBS Trust's business records.

The REMIC Trust Agreement or Pooling and Servicing Agreement (PSA) explicitly prohibits the Trustee from accepting any contribution of assets without the opinion of tax counsel to the effect of such contributions after the closing date and 90 days to correct or substitute date not having catastrophic consequences to the Trust. The closing date is the official start date of the REMIC and the date of execution of the Certificates.

REMIC Trusts must elect to become a Real Estate Mortgage Investment Conduit (REMIC) under Internal Revenue Service (IRS) code. This election is a mandatory and critical part of the legal issuance of Mortgage Backed Securities (MBS). The election will be printed and declared within the MBS Trust's official documents.

To qualify as a REMIC all interests in the entity itself must consist of one or more classes of regular interests and a single class of residual interests (860D). The interests must be issued on the startup day which is the closing date (IRS 860G-2).

The regular interest terms are fixed on the startup day (860G). Regular interests entitle holders to specified principal and interest payments at fixed or variable rates. Interests issued after the startup date do not qualify for regular interest REMIC status. Assets acquired, meaning mortgage loans, have the 90 days from startup date to be substituted, exchanged or purchased. After this, any loan acquisition is a prohibited transaction with potentially catastrophic tax consequences as identified previously in this chapter.

REMICs allow the mortgage backed security to have multiple classes of certificates. The interest and principal payments from mortgages are directed into different classes of separately traded securities. There can be any number of classes holding regular interests and one single class of residual interest. You will see evidence of this in a distribution report where it lists the classes in a spreadsheet format page after page.

Classes are commonly referred to by the French word for slices, *tranches*. REMIC level IRS formalities must be followed to qualify for the tax preferential pass-through treatment.

The residual interest class (or tranche) is an ownership interest that resembles equity more than debt, but can be either. Equity is ownership like stocks, debt is bond or debt style ownership. It can consist of rights of ownership in the REMIC pool of mortgage assets, subject to the claims of regular interest holders. Some rights to receive mortgage assets may exist under written agreement. Residual interest holders are the last to be paid.

Residual interest distributions are made on a pro rata basis, so that multiple holders of residual class interests are not considered multiple classes which would or could disqualify the REMIC under IRS rules. The risk of residual class holders not receiving cash flow is greater than other classes but the rewards of potential gains from equity interest in the holdings is greater. Issuers often retain the residual interest. All that is necessary to qualify as a residual class is to designate it as such when the REMIC starts up. In Agency MBS the residual class may be referred to as the "R" class.

Any number of regular classes or tranches can be included. They may be designated by letters or numbers or combinations of both. For example the "A" class or the "A-1" class will be the senior or first to be paid class.

REMICs may include a "Z" class where cash flow is only paid to the investor after all other classes were paid. The Z class accrues unpaid interest.

Classing or Tranching allows discretionary attributes to be allocated, thereby suiting individual investor needs. For example, there may be interest only classes, principal only classes, sequential pay classes, planned amortization classes, targeted amortization classes, companion classes, senior classes, mezzanine classes, junior classes, support classes. The list goes on… In short, REMICs can be classed or tranched into any number of classes suitable for the investors.

In MBS, the classes do not own specific mortgages, they own rights and entitlements in the groups of mortgages that make up the classes.

In the "mortgages in" stage, all the mortgages are received, reviewed for proper conveyance and documentation, then provided to an approved or designated Document Custodian who attests to their receipt and holds the properly endorsed and assigned blue ink originals. The investors are the "owners" and the document custodian for the Trustee is the "holder" of the Notes and Mortgages. In Agency MBS, Fannie Mae, Freddie Mac are the owners and holders, and they guarantee payments to the investors.

Some key points of the REMIC Rules

REMICs must start up on a particular day, often termed the Closing Date. The business activity of the REMIC is limited in MBS to holding a fixed pool of mortgages and distributing payments received to investors.

The MBS pool of mortgages is considered "static" to comply with the fixed pool of assets requirement. REMICs typically have a "cut-off date" that takes place prior to the closing date. This may be a few weeks to one month or so before the closing date and allows time to examine the mortgage loan asset acquisitions including conveyance and documentation.

Nitty Gritty of MBS © 2016 Richard M. Kahn

Movement of mortgage assets after the startup closing date is prohibited or strictly limited. We refer here to the IRS tax code period of 90 days from closing date (synonymous with startup date) as a designated period after the closing date in which "clean up" of mortgage assets may be made. This can include activities such as substituting like kind mortgages for defective or defaulted mortgages. So herein when the 90 day clean up is mentioned it refers to mortgage or loan asset clean up.

- This is not the "clean up call" referred to in 26 CFR 1.860G-2. The "clean up call" is the redemption of a class of regular interests whose prior payments and the costs associated outweigh the benefits of maintaining the class itself.

The startup day means the day on which the REMIC issues all of its regular and residual interests. The party who issues certificates to the MBS may contribute property to a REMIC in exchange for regular or residual interests over any 10 consecutive day period and the REMIC may designate any of those 10 days as its startup day. That day, when it is so designated, then becomes the official start up day and all interests are treated as issued on that day.

The date structure can look like this example:

>January 1: Cut-off date.

>January 31: Closing date.

>May 2: 90 days date within which to perform loan asset clean up including substitutions of defective loans, conveyance and loan documentation issues.

Business activity and cash contributions in the 90 days process of clean up that are not performed in the clean up period can have adverse consequences to the REMIC. For example, a 100% contributions tax on cash received, a 100% prohibited transactions tax, a 100% post loan modification tax in income or even worse; failure for the MBS to qualify or continue to qualify as a REMIC.

If a REMIC fails to qualify as a REMIC then double taxation will or could ensue each year and may be recaptured going back to the start-up date if the IRS finds out transactions occurred in previous years without reporting. In that case, the potential of additional fraud charges and penalties might apply if it was judged willful. Here is an example where an MBS REMIC can suffer the dire consequences mentioned in the paragraph above. For example, a REMIC buys or receives ten transferred defaulted loans worth $300,000 each for a total of $3 million in assets by business activity after the 90 day

Nitty Gritty of MBS © 2016 Richard M. Kahn

period. A 100% prohibited transaction tax on top of any interest tax could include a $3 million dollar additional tax due.

Any activity that could cause adverse consequences is dealt with in the MBS agreements. Most likely this is disclosed in the Pooling and Servicing Agreement (PSA), or Trust Agreement, or Prospectus. The action typically requires a majority vote of all Certificate holders, plus an outside independent legal tax opinion that the contemplated transaction will not jeopardize the REMIC status.

Public MBS REMIC Trusts that include certificates sold to the public require disclosure as per Regulation AB of the Securities and Exchange Commission during the first calendar year of their start-up. After this period issuers may file Form 15-D termination filings to end this. The filings are available to the public on SEC EDGAR. Attestations by well qualified corporations will specify that all the disclosures required have been filed, and that all the filings of master servicer and securities administrators are compliant.

Even the act of a simple loan modification can trigger the numerous technical requirements and result in adverse consequences for the REMIC.

IRS Guidance provided commercial REMICs with relaxed loan modification standards In September 2009. As a result of Mortgage Meltdown 2008 and millions of mortgage defaults, the U.S. Government realized the importance of loan modifications and so the IRS came out with modified guidance. This guidance provided commercial mortgages held in REMICs to receive relaxed loan modification standards that would not cause the IRS to challenge the tax status of the CMBS REMIC, "C" standing for Commercial.

Loan modifications in REMIC MBS are defined for the IRS by Treasury Regulations.[15] There are numerous issues. Modifying term or time is a modification, even if it occurs as a result of a Chapter 11 bankruptcy court plan that becomes effective. Change in yield (within certain parameters) is a significant modification. The general rule is that a significant modification must take into consideration a collection of IRS determinations. When taken collectively even the smallest changes can be deemed significant.

Flexibility of the changes in REMIC rules on modifications to modify loans without adverse tax consequences are based largely on whether the loan servicer reasonably believes there is a significant

---

[15] 26 C.F.R. § 1.1001-3 Modifications of debt instruments. Title 26 - Internal Revenue

risk of default or the loan is actually in default.

It is the primary master loan servicer that makes the decision. If so designated in a sub-servicing agreement the sub servicer can also make the decision. The loan modification documentation taken by a sub servicer must go to the primary master servicer. The Pooling and Servicing Agreement (PSA) designates this requirement and authority. The PSA designates the master servicer and whether a special defaulted (or imminent default) loan servicer will have responsibility. The PSA designates which if any of these servicers will work with a borrower to modify. Mostly, a special default loan servicer will be designated. The PSA may specify when and whether a defaulted loan goes to the default loan servicer.

In most REMIC MBS the Master Servicer represents the collective interests of the investors with the borrower. The Trustee has this responsibility with the MBS investors.

When loans default or become late enough to indicate imminent default, the Master Servicer is designated with the obligation to conclude if a loan modification or a foreclosure will produce the best results for the investors. Borrower's have no right to modify. Master Servicers are under written obligation to do what is best for the investors, without consideration of the borrower's interests. Servicers are not sentimental, they are bankers.

Defaulted loans or those facing imminent default may come under relaxed IRS rules that ease some of the REMIC prohibited transaction tax restrictions. In this manner those that might otherwise threaten the REMIC MBS may be excluded in specific instances. The master servicer decides.

Every REMIC is required to identify their mortgage pool assets individually. The Document Custodian is the party designated to have the holder in due course originals in their possession and will present them to the Master Servicer or designated party in a foreclosure action to prove holder and owner status. Sometimes a REMIC will designate the master servicer or trustee maintain the holder in due course originals.

REMICs pay the highest corporate rate for Federal and in some cases State taxes on foreclosure income. They report to the IRS on Form 1066, which is the U.S. Real Estate Mortgage Investment Conduit (REMIC) Income Tax Return. Schedule J provides the tax computation on net income from prohibited transactions and from foreclosure property. The total tax of Schedule J line 12 goes right onto the first page under Section II – Tax and Payments. So it is a direct 100% "hit" if REMIC status is removed from the MBS. This results is considered catastrophic. The instructions for Form 1066 reveal the key qualifications of the REMIC: start date, prohibited transactions, gain from dispositions of mortgages, gross income from foreclosure property, contributions after the startup date, residual interests and more.

The IRS requires designation of a Tax Matters Person (TMP). IRS reporting relies on the determination and reporting of tax to be performed by the party filing the tax return, or their designated accountant.

When a foreclosure takes place that jeopardizes the REMIC and the REMIC MBS is not party to the foreclosure transaction or proceeding, the REMIC TMP may not be reporting prohibited transactions properly. Public MBS can be examined on this matter. Activity in specific MBS of this class of prohibited transactions should be none.

Let's summarize key issues of REMIC Rules and then identify key REMIC Rules in pertinent part that apply to key REMIC issues.

A summary of key issues affecting MBS Securitization:
1. Transfer of a Defaulted Loan:

    a. The IRS REMIC tax code requires acquisition of "qualified mortgage loans". These are what the industry terms "performing loans".

2. Material changes to the loan pool

    a. The IRS REMIC tax code's requirement for passive loan pools results in the prohibition on material changes in the loan assets once it is in the REMIC pool and outside the closing date or 90 days to correct or substitute dates.

    b. Substitutions of like mortgages and mortgage terms can be made for up to 2 years from the Closing Date. After this 2 year period no loans can be substituted. Substitution after 90 days is often stipulated to be accompanied by a Tax Opinion placed on permanent file with the MBS distribution documents.

3. Adverse consequences include:

a. 100% prohibited transactions tax on any gain realized from the deemed disposition and in some circumstances

    i. Imposition of a 100% prohibited transaction tax; and

    ii. Failure of the entire REMIC to continue to qualify as a REMIC, thereby causing full double corporate taxation on all income derived from its mortgage assets pool.

The IRS REMIC Code, in Pertinent Part

26 C.F.R. REMIC Considerations

- Code snippets are in *italicized Times Roman* font.
- Expert comments have an arrow head next to them..

<u>Identifying the Full Code and Rules with Hypertext Links footnoted.</u>

➤ The IRS REMIC rules referenced in the SEC Documented Transaction filings are available to the public online. They are known as 26 <u>USCA § 860 A through G</u>.

- USCA stands for United States Code Annotated.
  - Title 26 is the Internal Revenue Code.
    - Subchapter M includes Regulated Investment Companies and Real Estate Investment Trusts

- Part IV references Real Estate Mortgage Investment Conduits (REMICS)

26 C.F.R.

Title 26: Internal Revenue

PART 1—INCOME TAXES[16]

Real Estate Investment Trusts[17]

➤ REMICS must acquire permitted assets (which I highlight in more detail below this snippet section). The party who sells the assets to the REMIC Trust is specified, as well as the dates and types of qualifying assets are a critical component.

§ 1.860D-1 Definition of a REMIC.

*(3) Asset test—(i) In general. For purposes of the asset test of section 860D(a)(4), substantially all of a qualified entity's assets are **qualified mortgages** and permitted investments if the qualified entity owns no more than a de minimis amount of other assets.*

§ 1.860F-2 Transfers to a REMIC.

(a) Formation of a REMIC—(1) In general. For Federal income tax purposes, a REMIC formation is characterized as the contribution

---

[16] http://law.justia.com/cfr/title26/26-9.0.1.1.1.html

[17] http://www.gpo.gov/fdsys/granule/CFR-2011-title26-vol1/CFR-2011-title26-vol1-sec1-58-6/content-detail.html

of assets by a sponsor (as defined in paragraph (b)(1) of this section) to a REMIC in exchange for REMIC regular and residual interests. If, instead of exchanging its interest in mortgages and related assets for regular and residual interests, the sponsor arranges to have the REMIC issue some or all of the regular and residual interests for cash, after which the sponsor sells its interests in mortgages and related assets to the REMIC, the transaction is, nevertheless, viewed for Federal income tax purposes as the sponsor's exchange of mortgages and related assets for regular and residual interests, followed by a sale of some or all of those interests. The purpose of this rule is to ensure that the tax consequences associated with the formation of a REMIC are not affected by the actual sequence of steps taken by the sponsor.

(b) Treatment of sponsor—(1) Sponsor defined. A sponsor is a person who directly or indirectly exchanges qualified mortgages and related assets for regular and residual interests in a REMIC. A person indirectly exchanges interests in qualified mortgages and related assets for regular and residual interests in a REMIC if the person transfers, other than in a nonrecognition transaction, the mortgages and related assets to another person who acquires a transitory ownership interest in those assets before exchanging them for

Nitty Gritty of MBS © 2016 Richard M. Kahn

interests in the REMIC, after which the transitory owner then transfers some or all of the interests in the REMIC to the first person.

➤ A REMIC is intended to be a passive investment in a static pool of mortgages. Because of its passive nature, a REMIC is limited as to how and when it can acquire mortgages. Here in pertinent part is a sampling of rules denoting what qualifies as an asset (ex. qualifying mortgages) and what does not qualify (ex. mortgages in default or going into default and timing of acquisition of the asset. In particular, a REMIC must in most cases acquire its mortgages within three months after its start-up. 26 U.S.C. § 860G(a)(3), (9).

§ 1.860G-2 Other rules.

(a) Obligations principally secured by an interest in real property—

(1) Tests for determining whether an obligation is principally secured. For purposes of section 860G(a)(3)(A), an obligation is principally secured by an interest in real property only if it satisfies either the test set out in paragraph (a)(1)(i) or the test set out in paragraph (a)(1)(ii) of this section.

(i) The 80-percent test. An obligation is principally secured by an interest in real property if the fair market value of the interest in real property securing the obligation—

Nitty Gritty of MBS © 2016 Richard M. Kahn

(A) Was at least equal to 80 percent of the adjusted issue price of the obligation at the time the obligation was originated (see paragraph (b)(1) of this section concerning the origination date for obligations that have been significantly modified); or

(B) Is at least equal to 80 percent of the adjusted issue price of the obligation at the time the sponsor contributes the obligation to the REMIC

(5) Obligations secured by an interest in real property. Obligations secured by interests in real property include the following: mortgages, deeds of trust, and installment land contracts; mortgage pass-thru certificates guaranteed by GNMA, FNMA, FHLMC, or CMHC (Canada Mortgage and Housing Corporation); other investment trust interests that represent undivided beneficial ownership in a pool of obligations principally secured by interests in real property and related assets that would be considered to be permitted investments if the investment trust were a REMIC, and provided the investment trust is classified as a trust under §301.7701–4(c) of this chapter; and obligations secured by manufactured housing treated as single family residences under section 25(e)(10) (without regard to the treatment of the obligations or the properties under state law).

*(f) Defective obligations—(1) Defective obligation defined. For purposes of sections 860G(a)(4)(B)(ii) and 860F(a)(2), **a defective obligation is a mortgage subject to any of the following defects**.*

*(i) **The mortgage is in default,** or a default with respect to the mortgage is reasonably foreseeable.*

(ii) The mortgage was fraudulently procured by the mortgagor.

(iii) The mortgage was not in fact principally secured by an interest in real property within the meaning of paragraph (a)(1) of this section.

(k) Startup day. The term "startup day" means the day on which the REMIC issues all of its regular and residual interests. A sponsor may, however, contribute property to a REMIC in exchange for regular and residual interests over any period of 10 consecutive days and the REMIC may designate any one of those 10 days as its startup day. The day so designated is then the startup day, and all interests are treated as issued on that day.

Nitty Gritty of MBS © 2016 Richard M. Kahn

Chapter 21

Conclusion

The explosive growth of Mortgage Backed Securitization created a
pervasive scenario. Mortgage loan ownership was unable to be
tracked as it had been in the traditional mortgage loan origination
model used successfully for hundreds of years.

MERS was organized and founded by the banks and Government
Sponsored Enterprises (GSEs), Fannie Mae and Freddie Mac. MERS
sidestepped the traditional recordation of mortgage ownership in the
county property recorder's office where the property was located.
MERS empowered lenders and loan servicer's employees instead, to
act like property recorder's offices. But these servicer's employees do
not have the integrity of a property recorder's office and
memorialized records dated from when they were originally filed.

This process questions the validity of loan ownership, rights and authority on some 30 million or more loans that find MERS on the mortgage.

Many banks, loan servicers and servicer document processing companies have been caught red-handed by the National Association Attorney Generals as well as multiple Federal Regulatory Agencies, conducting foreclosures in an unsafe and unsound manner.

A process that includes employing the practices of reverse engineering, otherwise known as backdating documents. Employees of these parties seeking to foreclose have been caught robo-signing, filing false affidavits and creating assignments of mortgages together with Notes to make it seem like mortgages were properly recorded and changed hands legally when they did not.

These actions have critical implications when the parties seeking to foreclose are not able to prove a party owns the loan they seek to foreclose.

MBS Securitization has complicated the matter because it involves multiple true sales in a complex process. True sales require properly recorded transfers of the Mortgage and Sales of the Note with properly evidenced endorsements on the Note, or by a permanently attached paper called an Allonge when there is no more room on the face of the note for endorsements.

A lawful foreclosure process requires precise legal steps to evidence ownership across multiple sales and parties. Failure to do so places ownership in critical doubt. Doubt not only of the rights and authority to foreclose but also of proving that mortgage loan ownership was actually transferred to MBS Trusts through the intervening ownership from the Originator to the MBS Trust. Not just in general, but on each and every specific mortgage assets the MBS Trust claims to have purchased in pools on the closing date of the MBS Trust. Also including any substitutions of mortgages that may have taken place afterwards, within the allowable window of time under REMIC Rules.

In traditional mortgage ownership terms, the title transfers in mortgages are "clouded" when there is a demonstrated inability to clearly determine ownership on the record.

Clear title in uncontestable form is at the foundation of America's real estate ownership market.

Nitty Gritty of MBS © 2016 Richard M. Kahn

Complicating matters further, with the advent of MBS Securitization beginning in 2000, mortgages were originated and then immediately or within a short time, turned into commodities and sold many times over. Based upon assessments in 2007 of credit default swaps, a vehicle of MBS mortgage resale, $1x of individual separate mortgages were sold $8x over. $62 trillion of credit default swaps in MBS mortgages was only at one point in time. It does not take into consideration multiple resales of the mortgages in the interim that occurred. Some have estimated that could have meant an individual $1x loan selling for $12x.

This process of selling the individual mortgages over and over for profits reveals that in the least, the originating lender was paid off in full on the mortgage loan. Interim traders in commodities trades do not take possession of the commodity, which in this case is an individual group on underlying mortgages. They trade the commodity derivatives for interim profits. Traders are not taking ownership of the loan and recording this action. They do not become lawful owners of the loan in a traditional real estate sense.

The lack of properly executed transfers in real estate ownership lays a questionable claim to legal ownership of a mortgage loan. It also brings into question the rights and authority of loan servicing, the

Nitty Gritty of MBS © 2016 Richard M. Kahn

right to receive payments from the borrower. Loan servicers that cannot demonstrate a chain of loan servicing agreements with a subsequent chain of owners that can demonstrate legal ownership, raises questions the servicer's legal right to receive payments from the borrowers.

It also creates a troublesome question when borrowers have made payments to servicers. Were the payments made to a servicer who could issue an unquestionable satisfaction of mortgage one day? We the payments made to a servicer acting for a true and lawful owner? Or was the servicer merely accepting payments on a loan that the servicer is unable to confirm a true and lawful owner?

These issues materially question the rights and authority of loan servicers in these circumstances seeking to foreclose, from even initiating that process. If neither the servicer nor party claiming ownership can demonstrate without a doubt that they have not paid money to purchase the particular mortgage and cannot demonstrate irrefutable chain of ownership, their legal ability to foreclose may be in question.

Exacerbating the problem is concern of allowing a party to foreclose who cannot demonstrate the ability to provide irrefutably clear

Nitty Gritty of MBS © 2016 Richard M. Kahn

satisfaction of mortgage passing clear title to the borrower when the loan is paid off.

When loan servicers and parties seeking to foreclose prefer to foreclose than modify a loan, rather seeking to have title passed to them on a property they cannot evidence lending money out on or proper ownership of by a party they represent, it further questions their legal rights to foreclose.

Courts are often asked to grant servicers and others claiming ownership the right to foreclose, but cannot demonstrate the legal right of ownership or willingness to modify a loan. When this right is granted by a Court these parties can then sell the property, evict the borrower, and keep the windfall proceeds for themselves.

Rarely do we find Courts granting disgorgement of profits to borrower's for providing a mortgage that was sold $8x over for profits.

Irregularities, falsities and misrepresentation in documentation of ownership rights and authority concerns arise from the MBS Securitization of mortgages in foreclosure actions and may provide a borrower remedies to contest foreclosure.

Nitty Gritty of MBS © 2016 Richard M. Kahn

Lenders and parties selling mortgage loans to MBS Trust investors have repurchase agreements in place with the MBS Trust. The same defects and discrepancies found by a borrower to undermine foreclosure are stipulated in the MBS Trust documents to require repurchase by sellers on loans sold to MBS Trusts. The claims of being an owner, coupled with the distinct inability to demonstrate either purchase or repurchase of a loan creates what are known as "bald claims" of ownership, as opposed to prima facie proof of ownership.

The foreclosure court is a precarious environment. Judges are in a hard place. Evaluating full compliance with applicable real estate foreclosure laws is not an easy undertaking. Failure of many borrower side attorneys to incorporate expert witnesses and their findings, facts and opinions into a case according to the well established rules of evidence enhances the difficulty Judges face.

Attorneys and parties to a legal action are unable to submit substantive evidence in their own cases as an expert would. They may only make claims and allegations. Finding a truly qualifying expert in this specialty is very difficult.

A cottage industry of pretender experts has arisen, claiming to endow a person with expert credentials after taking a one weekend 24 hour

Nitty Gritty of MBS © 2016 Richard M. Kahn

course, or a 14 hour primer. This is hardly the criteria upholding expert status. These pretender experts do not offer credible testimony into court. To the contrary, they regularly issue written testimony that violates the basic rules of evidence and expert witness testimony. When the time comes to require their personal appearance, they rarely appear. They charge clients fees for reporting but after the fact, do not provide expert oral testimony, deposition, voir dire, examination, cross-examination. Instead they are nowhere to be found when it comes time to taking a witness stand and put the "bulls eye" on themselves in a case.

In foreclosure, Judges decide whether an expert qualifies and whether their testimony and findings will be considered as evidence. Introducing pretender expert work in a case can be very detrimental if a Judge takes offense a the impudence of it.

It is therefore critically important in a contested foreclosure case to make sure that if you intend to submit an expert's facts, findings, documentation and testimony for consideration as evidence by a Judge, that is comes from a *real* highly qualifying expert, not a pretender expert. In this way a Judge may be enlightened to facts and findings and not alienated by them.

THE END

www.ingramcontent.com/pod-product-compliance
Lightning Source LLC
Chambersburg PA
CBHW071731270326
41928CB00013B/2637